SCARVES, SHRUGS, & SHAWLS

SCARVES, SHRUGS, & SHAWLS

22 knitted designs with
their special techniques

Sarah Hatton

Technical editor
Sharon Brant

ST. MARTIN'S GRIFFIN
NEW YORK

SCARVES, SHRUGS & SHAWLS

First US edition published in 2013
by St Martin's Press
175 Fifth Avenue,
New York NY 10010
www.stmartins.com

Created and produced by Berry & Bridges Ltd
Belsize Business Centre
258 Belsize Road
London NW6 4BT
UK

Library of Congress Cataloging-in-Publication Data
Available Upon Request

ISBN 978-1-250-02494-7

10 9 8 7 6 5 4 3 2 1

Printed in Singapore

CONTENTS

INTRODUCTION

Scarves, wraps, and shawls are the most perfect knitting projects as they are generally great to knit on the go and they are so easy to wear and use. A beautiful jewel-colored scarf is the ideal way to lift a plain outfit.

As a designer I am particularly drawn to lace and textured designs and I think this collection reflects those twin passions. It includes versatile designs encompassing every conceivable kind of scarf, wrap, shawl, or shrug. Rowan has such a beautiful range of yarns and colors that finding the perfect yarn and color palette to work with is really easy. The yarns in this book have something for every taste: they range from the finest cobweblike mohair/silk mix to chunky, cozy alpaca. With so many lace and textured stitches used in the patterns, I hope I have tried to offer plenty for knitters to experiment with and have some fun. For this reason it made perfect sense to work with the wonderful Sharon Brant, as she understands how to teach knitting techniques like no-one else. I hope you find the special techniques section which she put together (see pages 110–131) helpful and enlightening.

I have also included a section showing the different ways to wear and tie your finished projects (see pages 96–109), so that you can get the most from them in both style and practicality.

I hope you enjoy both knitting and wearing these projects as much as we did working on them.

Sarah Hatton

DESIGNS

This collection of versatile designs includes every conceivable kind of scarf, wrap, shawl, or shrug in yarns ranging from the finest mohair to warm and cozy alpaca. They also cover every possible form and stitch texture, so knitters can have a wonderful time experimenting with new techniques (for which there is more explanation on pages 110–131). A further section shows you how to vary the way they are worn or explains ways to tie them (see pages 96–109).

REVERSIBLE SHRUG

Knitted in warm and cozy Rowan *Lima*, this shrug is worked in all-over reversible cable rib (see page 120), meaning it has no right or wrong side, which is great on the tie detail.

See pattern, page 64.

TWO-WAY VEST

Knitted as a long cabled rectangle, with armholes, this simple construction also doubles up as a cozy scarf.
See pattern, page 76.

TRIANGULAR SCARF

With its decorative bobbles (see page 122) and simple stitch texture, this elegant design is knitted in Rowan *Wool Cotton 4ply*. *See pattern, page 58.*

LOOPED SCARF

This great textured scarf, knitted in soft Rowan
Lima, is joined to form a continuous loop.
See pattern, page 87.

HOODED SCARF

Chunky cables, knitted in Rowan *Baby Alpaca DK*, a cozy hood, and an extra-long length, make this a great choice for cold winter days.
See pattern, page 66.

CABLED WRAP

A cropped wrap top featuring delicate
cable patterns, this flattering design fastens
simply at the front with a brooch or pin.
Knitted in soft Rowan *Baby Alpaca DK*.
See pattern, page 78.

RUFFLE SCARF

Knitted in a mix of Rowan *Kidsilk Haze* and *Baby Alpaca DK*, this design has ribbons running throughout its length, so it can be worn either long as a scarf or ruched up around the neck for extra warmth.
See pattern, page 59.

FAIRISLE STOLE

This super-wide warm and cozy design
has an attractive Fairisle (see page 126)
decorative detail at each end. For different
ways to wear it, see How to Wear, page 100.
See pattern, page 74.

MOBIUS WRAP &
BEADED CORSAGE

With its unique twisted shape (created by
the Mobius shaping technique, see page
116), this little wrap-type scarf is knitted
in soft and luxurious Rowan *Kid Classic*.
The matching corsage is knitted in Rowan
Wool Cotton 4ply and *Kidsilk Haze*.
See patterns, pages 67 and 68.

LEAF DETAIL COLLAR

This pretty little collar (see Short-row shaping, page 114), with its bobble edging (see page 122) is worn with one end threaded through the garter stitch panel. Knitted in Rowan *Felted Tweed DK*. *See pattern, page 52.*

BEADED SCARF

Cool and sharp, this narrow beaded (see page 129) scarf could be dressed up or down. Learn how to tie it on page 108. Knitted in Rowan *Wool Cotton*. *See pattern, page 88.*

LOOP-STITCH COLLAR

Knitted in Rowan *Kidsilk Haze*, held double, sparkling beads add a touch of glamour (there is also a plain version of the pattern, see page 61). To create the shape, use the Short-row shaping technique on page 114.
See pattern, page 60.

INDULGENT WRAP

Generous and airy, this lacy wrap is
knitted in Rowan *Wool Cotton 4ply*. It is
started as a central square and worked
out to form the long ends. For help
working lace, see page 124.
See pattern, page 70.

CHEVRON SCARF

Clever combinations of colors in Rowan *Felted Tweed DK* create this lacy chevron pattern (knitted sideways). See page 98 for different ways to wear it.
See pattern, page 55.

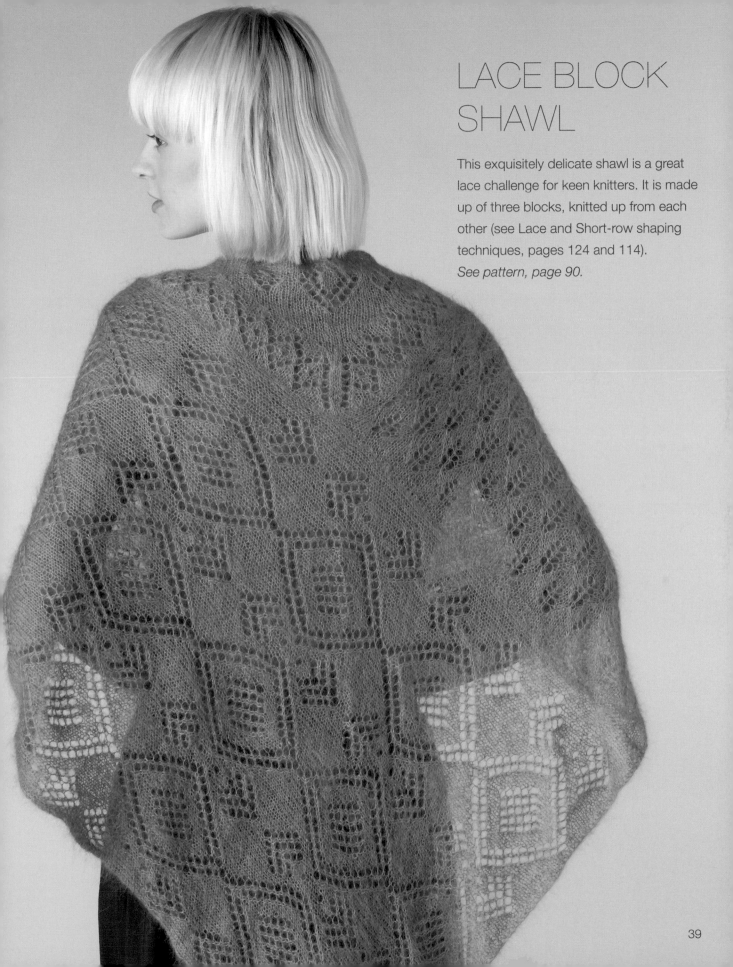

LACE BLOCK SHAWL

This exquisitely delicate shawl is a great lace challenge for keen knitters. It is made up of three blocks, knitted up from each other (see Lace and Short-row shaping techniques, pages 124 and 114).
See pattern, page 90.

MULTIWAY STOLE

Repeating panels of lace stitches in delicate Rowan *Kidsilk Haze* and *Fine Lace* held together, give this versatile stole its special character, and its button fastenings allow you to wear it in a variety of ways, such as a shrug, poncho, cape, or vest (see How to Wear, page 102).
See pattern, page 56.

BOLD STRIPE SCARF

This striking, simple-to-knit long scarf with its contrasting colored panels, is knitted in the round in Rowan *Kidsilk Haze*. See page 104 for how to wear it.
See pattern, page 54.

CRESCENT SHAWL
& SIMPLE
CORSAGE

This exquisite whisper of a shawl (see
Knitted-on edging technique, page 118)
and its matching corsage, are both knitted
in Rowan *Kidsilk Haze*.
See patterns, pages 62 and 81.

COLLARED CAPE

This pretty cape has lots of textural interest
to keep knitters hooked. It is knitted in soft
and cozy Rowan *Felted Tweed DK*.
See pattern, page 84.

FRILLED SHAWL

Knitted in Rowan *Wool Cotton* and *Kidsilk Haze*, using the special technique of Knitted-on edging (see page 118), this delicate shawl has great textural appeal. *See pattern, page 82.*

PATTERNS

This section includes all the patterns in the Gallery (pages 8–49). Each pattern specifies finished size, skill level, yarns, needles, and any extras required, as well as gauge and pattern notes or special abbreviations. For general abbreviations, see page 95. As most of the items are not fitted, gauge is not as crucial as for garments. Further information on the yarns used is given on page 134, and explanations of the special techniques included are given on pages 110–131.

LEAF DETAIL COLLAR

FINISHED SIZE

Approx 9 x 39½in/23 x 100cm

YARN

2 x 1¾oz/191yd balls of Rowan
Felted Tweed DK in Duck Egg 173

NEEDLES

Pair of size 5 (3.75mm) knitting
needles

GAUGE

23 sts and 30 rows to 4in/10cm over
St st using size 5 (3.75mm) needles
or size to obtain correct gauge.

SPECIAL TECHNIQUES

Short-row shaping, page 114
No-turn bobbles, page 122
Lace, page 124

SPECIAL ABBREVIATIONS

MB—make bobble by working k1, yo, k1, yo, k1 all into
next st, turn, p5, turn, k5, turn, p5, turn, skp, k1, k2tog,
turn, p3, turn, sk2p.

MSB—make small bobble by working k1, yo, k1 into next
st, turn, p3, turn, k3, turn, p3, turn, sk2p.

Wrap st—slip next st from left-hand needle onto right-
hand needle, taking yarn to opposite side of work between
the needles and then slipping the same st back onto left-
hand needle. When working back across this st you may
wish to pick up the wrapping loop with the wrapped st and
work together.

SCARF (make 2 pieces alike)

Cast on 51 sts.

Row 1 K1, * MB, k3, rep from * to last 2 sts, MB, k1.

Knit 3 rows.

Next row * K2tog, yo, rep from * to last st, k1.

Knit 3 rows.

Next row (RS) Knit.

Next row K2, purl to last 2 sts, k2.

These 2 rows set St st and g-st edging.

Work 16 rows more as set, ending with RS facing for
next row.

Next row K6, * sk2p, k6, rep from * to last 9 sts, sk2p,
k6. *41 sts.*

Knit 3 rows.

Next row * K2tog, yo, rep from * to last st, k1.

Knit 3 rows.

Next row K2, * p3, MSB, p2, rep from * to last 3 sts,
p1, k2.

Next row Knit.

Next row K2, * p2, MSB, p1, MSB, p1, rep from * to last
3 sts, p1, k2.

Knit 3 rows.

Next row * K2tog, yo, rep from * to last st, k1.

Knit 3 rows.

Work next 13 rows as set on chart, working central 12-st
rep 3 times, ending with WS facing for next row.

Knit 3 rows.

Next row * K2tog, yo, rep from * to last st, k1.

Knit 3 rows, inc 1 st at end of last row. *42 sts.*

Shape split

Next row * K1, slip next st onto stitch holder, rep from * to end. *21 sts.*

Working on these 21 sts only, work 29 rows in g st, ending with RS facing for next row.

Leave sts on a holder.

With RS facing, knit across the on 21 sts left on a holder.

Work 29 rows in g st, ending with RS facing for next row.

Next row * K1 from first holder, k1 from second holder, rep from * to end. *42 sts.*

Cont as foll:

Beg with a WS row and working in St st until work measures 4¾in/12cm, ending with RS facing for next row.

For left side only

Cont as foll:

**Row 1 Patt 35, wrap next st, and turn, work to end of row.

Row 3 Patt 29, wrap next st, and turn, work to end of row.

Row 5 Patt 23, wrap next st, and turn, work to end of row.

Row 7 Patt 17, wrap next st, and turn, work to end of row.

Work 2 rows.

Rep the last 10 rows 3 times more. **

Work 27 rows without shaping, ending with WS facing for next row.

Leave sts on a holder.

For right side only

Work 1 row.

Work as given for left side to **.

Work 26 rows without shaping, ending with WS facing.

With RS's of both pieces facing each other, bind off using the three-needle method.

Key

☐	knit on RS, purl on WS
●	purl on RS, knit on WS
╲	ssk
╱	k2tog
⋏	sk2p
○	yo
☐	pattern repeat

Chart

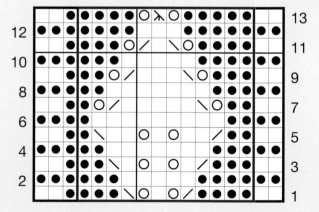

BOLD STRIPE SCARF

FINISHED SIZE

8 x 63in/20 x 160cm

NEEDLES

Size 6 (4mm) circular needle

YARN

1 x ⅞oz/229yd ball each of Rowan *Kidsilk Haze* in:

A—Candy Girl 606

B—Smoke 605

C—Trance 582

D—Marmalade 596

E—Jelly 597

GAUGE

21 sts and 27.5 rows to 4in/10cm measured over St st on size 6 (4mm) circular needle *or size to obtain correct gauge.*

SCARF

Cast on 84 sts.

Working in the round and St st throughout, cont in stripe patt as foll, working 44 rounds (6¼in/16cm) in each color.

Stripe pattern

Yarn A, yarn B, yarn C, yarn D, yarn E, yarn C, yarn B, yarn A, yarn E, yarn D.

Bind off.

SARAH SAYS

"We have shown this scarf in bright, jewel-like colors but it would also look very striking worked in a tight monochromatic palette. It can also be great fun to play around with different width stripes, as it will give your scarf a new look each time."

CHEVRON SCARF

FINISHED SIZE

12 x 73¼in/30 x 186cm

YARN

Rowan *Felted Tweed DK*

1 x 1¾oz/191yd ball each of:

A—Duck Egg 173

B—Paisley 171

E—Avocado 161

2 x 1¾oz/191yd balls each of:

C—Seafarer 170

D—Watery 152

NEEDLES

Size 5 (3.75mm) circular needle

GAUGE

23 sts and 32 rows to 4in/10cm over St st using size 5 (3.75mm) circular needle *or size to obtain correct gauge.*

SPECIAL TECHNIQUES

Lace, page 124

SCARF

Using A, cast on 427 sts.

Row 1 (RS) Using B, knit.

Row 2 K1, purl to last st, k1.

Row 3 K1, * [k2tog] 3 times, [yo, k1] 5 times, yo, [k2tog] 3 times, rep from * to last st, k1.

Row 4 Knit.

Rows 5 and 6 Using C, knit.

Rows 7 to 10 Using D, work as rows 1 to 4.

Rows 11 and 12 Using E, knit.

Rows 13 to 16 Using C, work as rows 1 to 4.

Rows 17 and 18 Using D, knit.

Rows 19 to 22 Using A, work as rows 1 to 4.

Rows 23 and 24 Using B, knit.

Rows 25 to 28 Using E, work as rows 1 to 4.

Rows 29 and 30 Using C, knit.

Rows 31 to 34 Using D, work as rows 1 to 4.

Rows 35 and 36 Using A, knit.

These 36 rows set patt.

Rep these 36 rows once more then rows 1 to 35 once more.

Using A, bind off knitwise.

SARAH SAYS

"When you first see the number of stitches to cast on it can look scary, but as the scarf is knitted lengthwise there aren't too many rows to knit to create the width. You could of course work more or fewer rows to create a narrower or wider scarf."

MULTIWAY STOLE

YARN

4(4:5:6:6) x ⅞oz/229yd balls of Rowan *Kidsilk Haze* in Meadow 581 (A)

3(3:3:3:4) x 1¾oz/437yd balls of Rowan *Fine Lace* in Patina 924 (B)

Note Use 1 end of each held together throughout

NEEDLES

Pair of size 7 (4.5mm) knitting needles

NOTIONS

10 buttons, ⅜in/10mm diameter

GAUGE

19 sts and 28 rows before blocking over St st on size 7 (4.5mm) needles *or size to obtain correct gauge.*

SPECIAL TECHNIQUES

Lace, page 124

MEASUREMENTS

	S	M	L	XL	XXL	
Width	19¾	19¾	19¾	24½	24½	in
	50	50	50	62	62	cm
Length	54¼	56¾	59	61½	63¾	in
	138	144	150	156	162	cm

STOLE

Cast on 93(93:93:117:117) sts.

Knit 4 rows.

Cont as foll:

Row 1 (RS) K2, yo, ssk, knit to last 4 sts, k2tog, yo, k2.

Row 2 K4, purl to last 4 sts, k4.

These 2 rows set edgings and should be worked throughout.

Row 3 K2, yo, ssk, k1, work 12 st rep as set on row of chart 7[7:7:9:9] times, k2tog, yo, k2.

This row sets chart placement.

Cont as set until row 40 of chart has been completed, ending with RS facing for next row.

Rep rows 41 to 44, 9[10:11:12:14] times.

Work rows 1 to 40 of chart.

Rep rows 41 to 44, 10[11:12:13:14] times.

Work rows 1 to 40 as set on chart, then rows 17 to 40 only.

Rep rows 41 to 44, 10[11:12:13:14] times.

Work rows 1 to 40 of chart.

Rep rows 41 to 44, 9[10:11:12:14] times.

Rep rows 1 to 42 of chart, ending with RS facing for next row.

Next row K2, yo, ssk, knit to last 4 sts, k2tog, yo, k2.

Knit 3 rows.

Bind off knitwise.

FINISHING

Soak and block to size (see page 63). Using Diagram 1 as a guide, sew on buttons to sides A and D. Place the first button approx 1in/2.5cm up from cast-on/bound-off edge and last approx 17¾in/45cm up from this point with remaining three buttons equally spaced between the two.

Chart

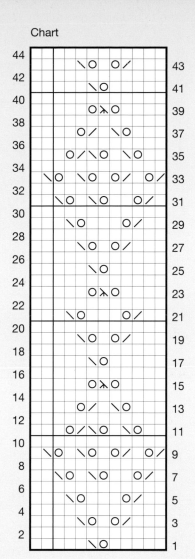

Key

☐	knit on RS, purl on WS
╲	ssk
╱	k2tog
⋏	sk2p
○	yo

Diagram 1

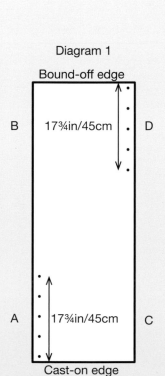

Bound-off edge

B   17¾in/45cm   D

A   17¾in/45cm   C

Cast-on edge

SARAH SAYS

"The fact that this design can be worn in so many ways means it's a really useful project to have in your closet. If the lace feels daunting, simply work in stockinette stitch making the most of the beautiful yarns."

TRIANGULAR SCARF

FINISHED SIZE

51 x 25½in/130 x 65cm

YARN

4 x 1¾oz/197yd balls of Rowan *Wool Cotton 4ply* in Leaf 491

NEEDLES

Pair of size 5 (3.75mm) knitting needles

GAUGE

19 sts and 32 rows to 4in/10cm over patt on size 5 (3.75mm) needles after light pressing, *or size to obtain correct gauge.*

SPECIAL TECHNIQUES

Provisional cast-on, page 112

No-turn bobbles, page 122

SPECIAL ABBREVIATIONS

MB—make bobble by working k1, yo, k1, yo, k1 all into next st, turn, p5, turn, k5, turn, p5, turn, skp, k1, k2tog, turn, p3, turn, sk2p.

SCARF

Using a provisional cast-on (see page 112), cast on 3 sts. Knit 10 rows.

Turn work through 90 degrees and pick up 5 sts along edge of this strip, then pull back provisional edging and work across these 3 sts. *11 sts.*

Row 1 K3, M1, k1, M1, place marker (to show spine of scarf, slip marker on every foll row), k3, M1, k1, M1, k3.

Row 2 K3, purl to last 3 sts, k3.

Row 3 [K3, M1] 4 times, k3.

Row 4 As row 2.

Row 5 K3, M1, k5, M1, k3, M1, k5, M1, k3.

Row 6 Knit.

Row 7 K3, M1, k7, M1, k3, M1, k7, M1, k3.

Row 8 As row 2.

Row 9 K3, M1, k9, M1, k3, M1, k9, M1, k3.

Row 10 As row 2.

Row 11 K3, M1, k11, M1, k3, M1, k11, M1, k3.

Row 12 Knit.

These 12 rows set patt.

Cont in patt as set, increasing 4 sts on every RS row until there are 339 sts, and ending with RS facing for next row.

Row 1 K3, M1, knit to marker, M1, k3, M1, knit to last 3 sts, M1, k3.

Row 2 Knit.

Rep these 2 rows 3 times more, dec 1 st at end of last row. *354 sts.*

Next row K4, * MB, k4, rep from * to last 4 sts, MB, k4. Bind off loosely. Press lightly.

RUFFLE SCARF

FINISHED SIZE

10¼ x 67¾in/26 x 172cm

NOTIONS

6yd/6m narrow ribbon

YARN

2 x ⅞oz/229yd balls of Rowan *Kidsilk Haze* in Majestic 589 (A)

2 x 1¾oz/109yd balls of Rowan *Baby Alpaca DK* in Cheviot 207 (B)

GAUGE

20 sts and 30 rows to 4in/10cm over St st using yarn A on size 5 (3.75mm) circular needle *or size to obtain correct gauge.*

NEEDLES

Size 5 (3.75mm) circular needle

SCARF

Using yarn A, cast on 514 sts.

** Beg with a K row, work 10 rows in St st, ending with RS facing for next row.

Change to yarn B.

Next row K1, * k2tog, k1, rep from * to end. *343 sts.*

Knit 3 rows.

Next row K2, * purl to last 2 sts, working yarn twice round needle for each stitch to create an elongated stitch, rep from * to last 2 sts, k2.

Next row K2, *slip next 3 sts onto right-hand needle dropping extra loops, slip these 3 sts back onto left-hand needle, and work (k1, p1, k1) into all sts together, rep from * to last 2 sts, k2.

Knit 4 rows.

Change to yarn A.

Next row (RS) K1, * inc in next st, k1, rep from * to end. *514 sts.*

Beg with a P row, work 1 row. **

Rep from ** to ** twice more.

Beg with a K row, work 8 rows in St st.

Bind off loosely.

Cut ribbon into three equal lengths. Thread a length through each band in B and knot ends to secure.

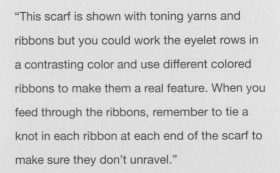

SARAH SAYS

"This scarf is shown with toning yarns and ribbons but you could work the eyelet rows in a contrasting color and use different colored ribbons to make them a real feature. When you feed through the ribbons, remember to tie a knot in each ribbon at each end of the scarf to make sure they don't unravel."

LOOP-STITCH COLLAR

FINISHED SIZE

Beaded version: 8in/20cm at widest
x 28½in/72cm

Plain version: 8in/20cm at widest x
33in/84cm

YARN

2 x ⅞oz/229yd balls of Rowan *Kidsilk
Haze* worked DOUBLE throughout:
Beaded version in Candy Girl 606
Plain version in Smoke 605

NOTIONS

Beaded version: approx 1,000 beads,
size 8

Plain version: hook-and-eye fasteners

NEEDLES

Pair of size 6 (4mm) knitting needles

GAUGE

17 sts and 27 rows to 4in/10cm over
loop st using yarn DOUBLE and size
6 (4mm) needles *or size to obtain
correct gauge.*

SPECIAL TECHNIQUES

Short-row shaping, page 114

Beading, page 129

SPECIAL ABBREVIATIONS

ML—make loop by knitting into next st but not slipping off
needle, bring yarn to front of work and wrap around thumb
before taking it to the back of the work and knitting into
the back of the same st. Slip st off needle and pass first st
over second.

MLB—make loop with bead by knitting into next st but not
slipping off needle, bring yarn to front of work and wrap
around thumb ensuring there is a bead on this length of
yarn before taking it to the back of the work and knitting
into the back of the same st. Slip st off needle and pass
first st over second.

Wrap st—slip next st from left-hand needle onto right-
hand needle, taking yarn to opposite side of work between
the needles and then slipping the same st back onto left-
hand needle. When working back across this st you may

wish to pick up the wrapping loop with the wrapped st and
work together.

NOTE

There are two versions of this pattern, a beaded version
and a plain version, without beads. Before you start
knitting you will need to thread beads onto one ball of the
yarn, see page 129. For the beaded version, use 1 end of
the ball of yarn threaded with beads held together with 1
end of the other ball. For the plain version, use 1 end from
each ball of yarn held together throughout.

COLLAR

Right-hand side

Cast on 3 sts.

Knit 2 rows.

Row 3 (RS) Inc in first st, ML or MLB, k1.

Row 4 and all foll alt rows Knit.

Row 5 [K1, ML or MLB] twice.

Row 7 Inc in first st, k1, ML or MLB, k1. *5 sts.*

Row 9 [ML or MLB, k1] twice, ML or MLB.

Row 11 Inc in 1st st, [ML or MLB, k1] twice.

These rows set placement of loops and increases.

Working in patt as set, inc 1 st at beg of 2 foll 4th rows then on every foll alt row to 33 sts.

Cont without shaping until work measures 12½in/32cm for beaded version, 15in/38cm for plain version, ending with RS facing for next row.

Next 2 rows Patt 25, wrap next st, turn, and knit to end.

Next 2 rows Patt 20, wrap next st, turn, and knit to end.

Next 2 rows Patt 15, wrap next st, turn, and knit to end.

Next 2 rows Patt 10, wrap next st, turn, and knit to end.

Next 2 rows Patt 5, wrap next st, turn, and knit to end.

Work 2 rows.

Leave sts on a holder.

Left-hand side

Cast on 3 sts.

Knit 2 rows.

Row 3 (RS) K1, ML or MLB, inc in last st.

Row 4 and all foll alt rows Knit.

Row 5 [ML or MLB, k1] twice.

Row 7 K1, ML or MLB, k1, inc in last st. *5 sts.*

Row 9 [ML or MLB, k1] twice, ML or MLB.

Row 11 [K1, ML or MLB] twice, inc in last st.

These rows set placement of loops and increases.

Working in patt as set, inc 1 st at end of 2 foll 4th rows then on every foll alt row to 33 sts.

Cont without shaping until work measures 12½in/32cm for beaded version, 15in/38cm for plain version, ending with WS facing for next row.

Next 2 rows Knit 25, wrap next st, turn, and patt to end.

Next 2 rows Knit 20, wrap next st, turn, and patt to end.

Next 2 rows Knit 15, wrap next st, turn, and patt to end.

Next 2 rows Knit 10, wrap next st, turn, and patt to end.

Next 2 rows Knit 5, wrap next st, turn, and patt to end.

Work 2 rows.

Leave sts on a holder.

FINISHING

With RS's of both pieces facing each other, bind off using the three-needle method.

Beaded version: make 2 twisted cords each approx 14in/35cm long and attach to cast-on edges.

Plain version: attach hook-and-eye fasteners approx 1in/2.5cm up from cast-on edge.

VARIATION: Plain version without beads

CRESCENT SHAWL

FINISHED SIZE

65¾ x 6¾in/167 x 17cm at narrowest and 13½in/34cm at widest point

YARN

2 x ⅞oz/229yd balls of Rowan *Kidsilk Haze* in Dewberry 600

NEEDLES

Pair of size 7 (4.5mm) knitting needles

GAUGE

17 sts and 33 rows before blocking over garter stitch on size 7 (4.5mm) needles *or size to obtain correct gauge.*

SPECIAL TECHNIQUES

Knitted-on edging, page 118

Lace, page 124

SPECIAL ABBREVIATIONS

Wrap st—slip next st from left-hand needle onto right-hand needle, taking yarn to opposite side of work between the needles and then slipping the same st back onto left-hand needle. When working back across this st you may wish to pick up the wrapping loop with the wrapped st and work together.

SHAWL

MAIN PART

Cast on 241 sts loosely.

Knit 2 rows.

Next row (RS) *K2tog, yo, rep from * to last st, k1.

Knit 1 row.

Next row K106, work next 29 sts as set on row 1 of Chart A, knit to end.

This row sets chart placement.

Working in 24-row rep as set on chart throughout, noting that only RS rows are noted on chart with all WS rows being worked in g st.

Patt 1 row.

Start shaping

Next row Patt 139, wrap next st, and turn.

Next row Patt 37, wrap next st, and turn.

Next row Patt 41, wrap next st, and turn.

Next row Patt 45, wrap next st, and turn.

Next row Patt 49, wrap next st, and turn.

Next row Patt 53, wrap next st, and turn.

Next row Patt 57, wrap next st, and turn.

Next row Patt 61, wrap next st, and turn.

Next row Patt 65, wrap next st, and turn.

Next row Patt 69, wrap next st, and turn.

Next row Patt 73, wrap next st, and turn.

Next row Patt 77, wrap next st, and turn.

Next row Patt 81, wrap next st, and turn.

Next row Patt 85, wrap next st, and turn.

Next row Patt 89, wrap next st, and turn.

Next row Patt 93, wrap next st, and turn.

Next row Patt 97, wrap next st, and turn.

Next row Patt 101, wrap next st, and turn.

Next row Patt 106, wrap next st, and turn.

Next row Patt 111, wrap next st, and turn.

Next row Patt 116, wrap next st, and turn.

Cont to work in g st only, working 5 more sts on each row between each wrap st until the foll row has been completed:

Next row Patt 231, wrap next st, and turn, patt to end.

EDGING

Next row On same needle as remaining sts, cast on 22 sts, knit 21 of these sts then k2tog last st with 1 st from main part of shawl.

You may wish to place a marker at this point as the number of stitches in the edging will alter throughout.

Row 1 (RS) Work as set on row 1 of Chart B.

Row 2 Work row 2 of chart B, k2tog last st with next st from main part of shawl.

These 2 rows set chart placement and decreasing of main part of shawl.

Cont as set until all but 1 st of the main part have been used, then bind off rem sts.

FINISHING

Soak the shawl in cold water. Remove and roll in a towel to remove most of the water. Pin out shawl to the size given and let dry.

Chart A

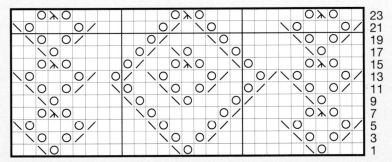

Key

☐	knit on RS
●	knit on WS
╲	ssk
╱	k2tog
⅄	sk2p
○	yo
☐	pattern repeat

Chart B: Edging

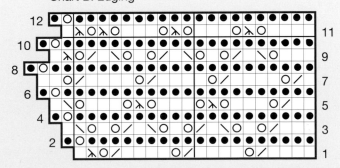

REVERSIBLE SHRUG

YARN

7(9:11:13) x 1¾oz/109yd balls of
Rowan *Lima* in La Paz 891

NEEDLES

Pair of size 9 (5.5mm) knitting
needles
Cable needle (CN)

GAUGE

30.5 sts and 26.5 rows to 4in/10cm
over patt using size 9 (5.5mm)
needles *or size to obtain correct
gauge*.

SPECIAL TECHNIQUES

Cables, page 120

MEASUREMENTS

	S	M	L	XL	
Width	17	20	23¼	26½	in
	43	51	59	67	cm
Length (with tie)	15	16	17½	18½	in
	38	41	44	47	cm

SPECIAL ABBREVIATIONS

C12ribF—slip next 6 sts onto CN and hold at front of
work, [k1, p1] 3 times, then [k1, p1] 3 times from CN.

C8ribF—slip next 4 sts onto CN and hold at front of work,
[k1, p1] twice, then [k1, p1] twice from CN.

C12ribB—slip next 6 sts onto CN and hold at back of
work, [k1, p1] 3 times, then [k1, p1] 3 times from CN.

C8ribB—slip next 4 sts onto CN and hold at back of work,
[k1, p1] twice, then [k1, p1] twice from CN.

SHRUG

Using size 9 (5.5mm) needles, cast on
132(156:180:204) sts.

Row 1 (RS) * K1, p1, rep from * to end.

Row 2 * K1, p1, rep from * to end.

These 2 rows set rib.

Work 6 rows more in rib.

Place marker.

Working in 8 row patt as set on chart, rep center 12 sts
9(11:13:15) times.

Cont as set until work measures approx 11(12¼:13½:14½)
in/28(31:34:37)cm, ending with row 2 of patt.

Split for fronts

Next row (RS) Patt 60(72:84:96), bind off 12 sts, patt to
end. *60(72:84:96) sts.*

Next row Patt first 12 sts as set on row 4 of chart, rep
center 12 sts 3(4:5:6) times, patt last 12 sts.

This row sets new chart placement.

Working on these sts only for first half, cont in patt until
front matches back to marker, ending with row 1 of patt
and WS facing for next row.

Work 8 rows in rib.

Bind off in rib.

Rejoin yarn to rem sts and work to match first front.

Working in mattress st and taking only half a st, join side seam to first cable twist.

Tie detail

Cast on 36 sts.

Work 8 rows in rib as set on back.

Working in 8 row patt as set on chart, rep center 12 sts once, cont as set until work measures approx 15¾(17:18:19¼)in/40(43:46:49)cm.

Place a marker at end of last row (you may also wish to note which row you ended on to match second tie).

Cont in patt until band fits around lower edge.

Place marker and cont in patt until work measures 8 rows less than first tie length from marker and ending with row 1 and WS facing for next row.

Work 8 rows in rib.

Bind off in rib.

Sew tie detail in place on shrug.

Key

☐ knit on RS, purl on WS

● purl on RS, knit on WS

C8ribB

C8ribF

C12ribF

C12ribB

☐ pattern repeat

Chart

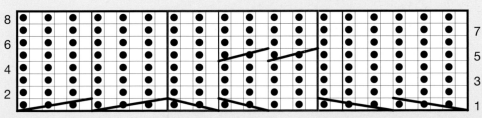

HOODED SCARF

FINISHED SIZE

12½ x 39½in/32 x 100cm

YARN

10 x 1¾oz/109yd balls of Rowan
Baby Alpaca DK in Southdown 208

NEEDLES

Pair of size 3 (3.25mm) knitting
needles

Pair of size 6 (4mm) knitting needles
Cable needle (CN)

GAUGE

28.5 sts and 32 rows to 4in/10cm
over patt on size 6 (4mm) needles *or
size to obtain correct gauge.*

SPECIAL TECHNIQUES

Cables, page 120

SPECIAL ABBREVIATIONS

C4B—slip next 2 sts onto CN and hold at back of work,
k2, then k2 from CN.

C4F—slip next 2 sts onto CN and hold and front of work,
k2, then k2 from CN.

T4B—slip next 2 sts onto CN and hold at back of work, k2,
then p2 from CN.

T4F—slip next 2 sts onto CN and hold at front of work, p2,
then k2 from CN.

SCARF (make 2 alike)

Using size 3 (3.25mm) needles, cast on 82 sts.

Knit 5 rows.

Next row (WS) K5, M1, [k8, M1] 4 times, k7, [M1, k8]
4 times, M1, k6. *92 sts.*

Change to size 6 (4mm) needles and cont as foll:

Row 1 K2, work row 1 as set on chart, then work sts
11–26 once more, k2.

Row 2 Knit and purl all sts as they present themselves.

These 2 rows set chart placement and g-st edgings.

Cont as set until work measures approx 39½in/100cm,
ending with row 23 of patt and WS facing for next row.

With RS's of both pieces facing each other, bind off using
the three-needle method.

Join back of head seam for 10in/25cm.

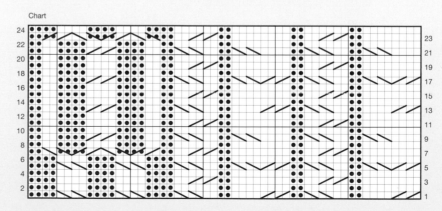

Key

☐ knit on RS, purl on WS

● purl on RS, knit on WS

C4B

C4F

T4F

T4B

MOBIUS WRAP

FINISHED SIZE

Approx 37 x 9½in/94 x 24cm

YARN

2 x 1¾oz/153yd balls of Rowan *Kid Classic* in Canard 871

NEEDLES

Size 8 (5mm) 40in/100cm long circular needle

GAUGE

17 sts and 28 rows to 4in/10cm over patt using size 8 (5mm) circular needle *or size to obtain correct gauge*.

SPECIAL TECHNIQUES

Mobius shaping, page 116

WRAP

Cast on 168 sts using the backward loop technique, then with the sts on a cable wire, pick up and knit 1 st in the loop between the first and second cast-on sts to close the gap and create a loop. Cont picking up in this way to the last st, pick up 1 st from the bottom of this last st. *336 sts*.

Place marker to denote start of round. For each round work a row in each direction with the cast on sitting in the middle of the mobius.

Round 1 Knit.

Round 2 Purl.

Round 3 Knit.

Round 4 * K4, p4, rep from * to end.

Round 5 * P1, k4, p3, rep from * to end.

Round 6 * P2, k4, p2, rep from * to end.

Round 7 * P3, k4, p1, rep from * to end.

Round 8 * P4, k4, rep from * to end.

Round 9 As round 4.

Round 10 * K3, p4, k1, rep from * to end.

Round 11 * K2, p4, k2, rep from * to end.

Round 12 * K1, p4, k3, rep from * to end.

Round 13 As round 8.

Round 14 Knit.

Round 15 Purl.

Round 16 Knit.

Round 17 Purl.

These 17 rounds set patt.

Rep these 17 rounds once.

Next round Knit.

Next round Purl.

Bind off.

BEADED CORSAGE

FINISHED SIZE

5in/13cm diameter

YARN

1 x 1¾oz/197yd ball each of Rowan
Wool Cotton 4ply in:

A—Hedge 494

B—Celanden 482

1 x ⅞oz/229yd ball of Rowan *Kidsilk
Haze* in Trance 582 (C)

NEEDLES

Pair of size 3 (3.25mm) knitting
needles

Pair of size 6 (4mm) knitting needles

NOTIONS

Beads in two colors: 57 x color A,
94 x color B

Brooch finding

GAUGE

28 sts and 36 rows to 4in/10cm over
St st using size 3 (3.25mm) needles
or size to obtain correct gauge.

SPECIAL TECHNIQUES

Beading, page 129

SPECIAL ABBREVIATIONS

PB—Place bead by bringing yarn to front (RS) of work and
slipping the bead up next to st just worked, slip next st
purlwise from left needle to right needle before taking yarn
back to back (WS) of work, leaving bead sitting in front of
the slipped st on RS.

NOTE

Before starting to knit, thread beads onto yarn, see page 129.

CORSAGE

CENTER SECTION

Thread 57 beads in color A onto yarn A.

Using size 3 (3.25mm) needles and yarn A, cast on 13 sts.

Row 1 K1, * PB but using 5 beads instead of 1, k1, rep
from * to end.

Row 2 K1, * inc in next st, k1, rep from * to end. *19 sts.*

Row 3 K1, * PB but using 3 beads instead of 1, k1, rep
from * to end.

Row 4 As row 2. *28 sts.*

Row 5 Knit.

Row 6 * Inc in next st, k1, rep from * to end. *42 sts.*

Row 7 Knit.

Row 8 Purl.

Bind-off row Bind off 2 sts, * slip st back onto left-hand
needle, [take yarn over left-hand needle, then pass the st
over this loop] 3 times, bind off 2 sts, rep from * to end.
Join side seam and work gathering sts around center and
gather slightly. Fasten off.

OUTER SECTION

Thread 42 beads in color B onto yarn B.

Using size 3 (3.25mm) needles and yarn B, cast on
100 sts.

Row 1 K2, * yo, bind off 5 sts (1 st left on needle), k1, rep
from * to end. *44 sts.*

Knit 1 row.

Row 3 * K1, PB, rep from * to last 2 sts, k2.

Row 4 P1, * PB, p1, rep from * to last st, p1.

Row 5 Knit.

Row 6 Purl.

Row 7 K1, * k4, k2tog, rep from * to last st, k1.

Purl 1 row.

Row 9 K1, * k3, k2tog, rep from * to last st, k1.

Purl 1 row.

Row 11 K1, * k2, k2tog, rep from * to last st, k1.

Purl 1 row.

Row 13 K1, * k1, k2tog, rep from * to last st, k1.

Purl 1 row.

Row 15 K2tog to end.

Break off yarn, thread through rem sts, and fasten off.

POMPOM BACKGROUND

Using size 6 (4mm) needles and yarn C, cast on 7 sts.

Row 1 (RS) * K1, yo, rep from * to last st, k1. *13 sts.*

Row 2 and every foll alt row Purl.

Row 3 * K2, yo, rep from * to last st, k1. *19 sts.*

Row 5 * K3, yo, rep from * to last st, k1. *25 sts.*

Row 7 * K4, yo, rep from * to last st, k1. *31 sts.*

Cont to inc in this way until the foll row has been completed: * k16, yo, rep from * to last st, k1.

Work 3 rows in St st.

Next row * K17, yo, rep from * to last st, k1.

Work 3 rows in St st.

Bind off.

RIBBON DETAIL 1

Thread 32 beads in color B onto yarn B.

Using size 3 (3.25mm) needles, yarn A, and thumb method if possible, cast on 50 sts.

Using yarn B, cont as foll:

Row 1 and every foll RS row Knit.

Row 2 K2, p2, [pb, p3] 8 times, purl to last 2 sts, k2.

Row 4 K2, p1, [pb, p1] 16 times, purl to last 2 sts, k2.

SARAH SAYS ∘○○

"A little corsage can be a great way to use up oddments of yarn and can add a really striking detail when wearing your scarf or shawl. They also make great gifts!"

Row 6 As row 2.

Row 7 Using yarn A, knit.

Using yarn A, bind off knitwise on WS.

RIBBON DETAIL 2

Thread 20 beads in color B onto yarn B.

Using size 3 (3.25mm) needles, yarn A, and thumb method if possible, cast on 38 sts.

Using yarn B, cont as foll:

Row 1 and every foll RS row Knit.

Row 2 K2, p2, [PB, p3] 5 times, purl to last 2 sts, k2.

Row 4 K2, p1, [PB, p1] 10 times, purl to last 2 sts, k2.

Row 6 As row 2.

Row 7 Using yarn A, knit.

Using yarn A, bind off knitwise on WS.

FINISHING

Join side seam of pompom background section. Work a row of gathering sts around the outer edge, pull tight, and fasten off. This gathered edge will form the center front of the pompom.

Place center section on top of outer section, then place this in the center of the pompom section and sew in position. Sew the two ribbon strips in place behind pompom, making sure to hide sections where there are no beads. Attach brooch finding.

INDULGENT WRAP

FINISHED SIZE

15¾ x 94½in/40 x 240cm

YARN

8 x 1¾oz/197yd balls of Rowan
Wool Cotton 4ply in Celanden 482

NEEDLES

Pair of size 6 (4mm) knitting needles

For circular method version

Size 6 (4mm) circular needle

Set of size 6 (4mm) double-pointed
knitting needles (DPN)

GAUGE

22 sts and 30 rows to 4in/10cm
measured over patt on size 6 (4mm)
needles when lightly pressed *or size
to obtain correct gauge*.

SPECIAL TECHNIQUES

Knitted-on edging, page 118

Lace, page 124

Picking up stitches for edgings, page 130

SPECIAL ABBREVIATIONS

Cluster 3—(with yarn at front, slip next 3 sts onto right-
hand needle, take yarn to back of work and slip 3 sts back
onto left-hand needle), with yarn at front slip next 3 sts
onto right-hand needle.

CENTER SECTION

For two needle method

Cast on 9 sts.

Row 1 [K1, yo] 8 times, k1. *17 sts.*

Row 2 Purl.

Row 3 K1, [yo, k3, yo, k1] 4 times. *25 sts.*

Row 4 Purl.

Row 5 K1, [yo, k5, yo, k1] 4 times. *33 sts.*

Row 6 Purl.

Row 7 K1, [work row 1 of Chart A, k1] 4 times.

Row 8 and every foll alt row Purl.

Row 9 K1, [work row 3 of Chart A, k1] 4 times.

Row 11 K1, [work row 5 of Chart A, k1] 4 times.

Rows 7 to 11 set chart placement and increases.

Cont from chart until row 72 is completed, ending with RS

facing for next row. *321 sts.*

For circular method

Cast on 8 sts and spread evenly between DPN. Change to
circular needle when there are too many sts to work
on DPN.

Round 1 [K1, yo] 8 times. *16 sts.*

Round 2 Knit.

Round 3 [K1, yo, k3, yo] 4 times. *24 sts.*

Round 4 Knit.

Round 5 [K1, yo, k5, yo] 4 times. *32 sts.*

Round 6 Knit.

Round 7 K1, [work row 1 of Chart A, k1] 3 times, work row
1 of Chart A.

Round 8 and every foll alt round Knit.

Round 9 K1, [work row 3 of Chart A, k1] 3 times, work row

3 of Chart A.

Round 11 K1, [work row 5 of Chart A, k1] 3 times, work row 5 of Chart A.

Rounds 7 to 11 set chart placement and increases.

Cont from chart until row 72 is completed, ending with RS facing for next row. *320 sts.*

For both versions

Next row Bind off 80 sts, k40, M1, k40, turn, and leave rem sts on a holder and cont on these 81 sts only.

Working in rows not rounds, cont as foll:

Next row Purl.

Beg with a K row, work 2 rows in St st, ending with RS facing for next row.

Next row K4, work next 9 sts as set on row 1 of Chart B, k3, work next 49 sts as set on row 1 of Chart C, k3, work next 9 sts as set on row 1 of Chart B, k4.

Next row Purl.

Next row K4, work next 9 sts as set on row 3 of Chart B, k3, work next 49 sts as set on row 3 of Chart C, k3, work next 9 sts as set on row 3 of Chart B, k4.

Next row Purl.

These 4 rows set chart placement.

Cont in patt as set, working rows 1 to 8 of Chart C once, then rows 9 to 36 three times, then rows 37 to 48 once, ending with RS facing for next row.

Cont as foll:

Row 1 K4, work next 9 sts as appropriate row of Chart B, k55, work next 9 sts as appropriate row of Chart B, k4.

Row 2 Purl.

Rep these 2 rows once.

Row 5 K4, work next 9 sts as appropriate row of Chart B, k2, [yo, sk2p, yo, k3] 8 times, yo, sk2p, yo, k2, work next 9 sts as appropriate row of Chart B, k4.

Row 6 Purl.

Row 7 K4, work next 9 sts as appropriate row of Chart B,

k2, [k3, yo, sk2p] 8 times, k5, work next sts as appropriate row of Chart B, k4.

Row 8 Purl.

Rep last 4 rows 3 times more, then first 2 rows once more.

Work rows 1 to 4 once more.

Next row K4, work next 9 sts as set on appropriate row of Chart B, k3, work next 49 sts as set on row 1 of Chart C, k3, work next 9 sts as set on appropriate row of Chart B, k4.

Next row Purl.

Next row K4, work next 9 sts as set on appropriate row of Chart B, k3, work next 49 sts as set on row 3 of Chart C, k3, work next 9 sts as set on appropriate row of Chart B, k4.

Next row Purl.

These 4 rows set chart placement.

Cont in patt as set, working rows 1 to 8 of Chart C once, then rows 9 to 36 3 times, then rows 37 to 48 once, ending with RS facing for next row.

Work 4 rows in St st, ending with RS facing for next row.

Cont in patt as set on Chart D until chart row 84 is completed, ending with RS facing for next row.

Knit 1 row.

Bind off knitwise on WS.

Working on rem sts, with RS facing, bind off until there are 80 sts left, k40, M1, k40. *81 sts.*

Complete to match first side of wrap.

EDGING

Sewn-on version

Cast on 6 sts.

Row 1 (WS) K1, yo, k2tog, k2, [yo] twice, k1.

Row 2 K1, [k1, k1tbl] into double yo of previous row, k2tog, yo, k3.

Row 3 K1, yo, k2tog, k5.

Row 4 Bind off 2 sts (1 st left on needle), k2tog, yo, k3.

These 4 rows set patt.

Cont in patt until edging fits along entire side edge of shawl when slightly stretched.

Slip st in position.

Work second side to match.

Knitted-on version

Cast on 6 sts, with RS facing, pick up st from edge of shawl and pass last st of edging over this st (this joins the edging and border sts).

Row 1 (WS) K1, yo, k2tog, k2, [yo] twice, k1.

Row 2 K1, [k1, k1tbl] into double yo of previous row,

k2tog, yo, k3, with RS facing pick up st from edge of shawl and pass last st of edging over this st.

Row 3 K1, yo, k2tog, k5.

Row 4 Bind off 2 sts (1 st left on needle), k2tog, yo, k3, with RS facing pick up st from edge of shawl and pass last st of edging over this st.

Cont in this way until edging has been worked all the way up side of shawl, ending with RS facing for next row.

Bind off.

Work second side to match.

NOTE I would recommend picking up 1 st to every 2 rows (see page 130).

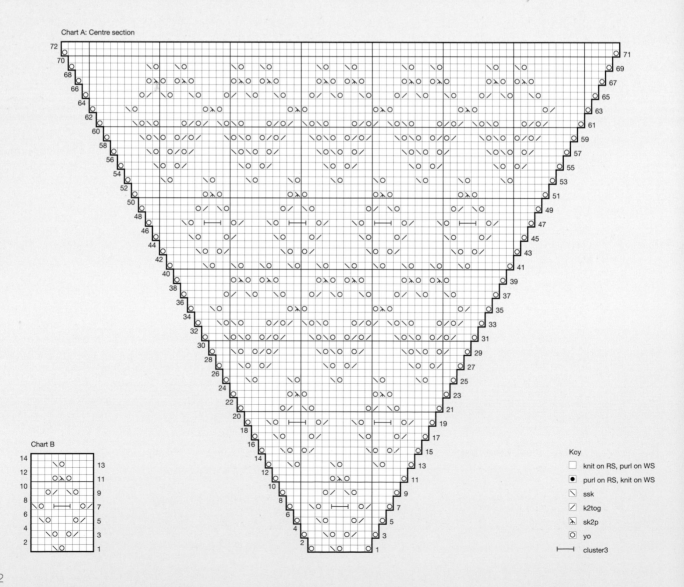

Chart A: Centre section

Chart B

Key

☐ knit on RS, purl on WS

● purl on RS, knit on WS

◸ ssk

◹ k2tog

人 sk2p

○ yo

├──┤ cluster3

Chart D

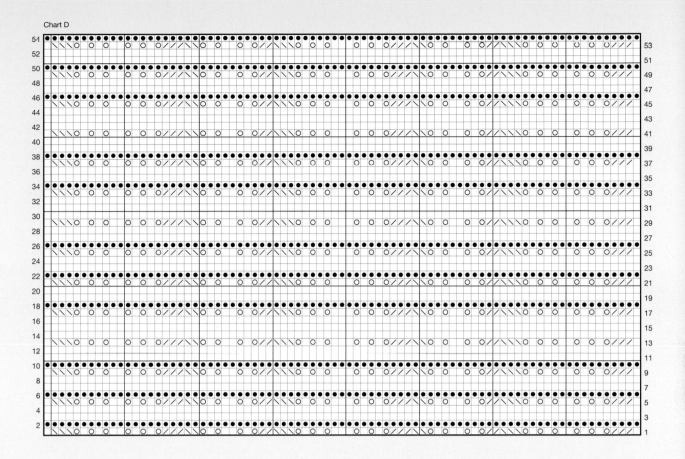

Chart C

FAIRISLE STOLE

FINISHED SIZE

18½ x 69¼in/47 x 176cm

YARN

Rowan *Felted Tweed DK*

6 x 1¾oz/191yd balls of

Camel 157 (A)

1 x 1¾oz/191yd balls each of:

B—Carbon 159

C—Rage 150

D—Seasalter 178

E—Avocado 161

NEEDLES

Pair of size 5 (3.75mm) knitting

needles

GAUGE

25 sts and 29 rows to 4in/10cm

over patterned St st using size 5

(3.75mm) needles *or size to obtain

correct gauge.*

SPECIAL TECHNIQUES

Fairisle, pages 126–128

STOLE

Using A, cast on 117 sts.

Row 1 K1, * p1, k1, rep from * to end.

Row 2 * P1, k1, rep from * to last st, p1.

Row 3 As row 2.

Row 4 As row 1.

These 4 rows set double seed st patt.

Work 8 rows more in patt.

Next row Patt 7, knit to last 7 sts, patt 7.

Next row Patt 7, purl to last 7 sts, patt 7.

These 2 rows set St st and double seed-st edging.

Work 8 rows more as set.

Cont as foll:

** Row 1 Patt 7, work next 103 sts as set on row 1 of

chart, patt 7.

This row sets chart placement.

Work until all 54 rows of chart have been completed,

ending with RS facing for next row.

Work rows 1 to 19 as set on chart, ending with WS facing

for next row. **

Beg with a WS row, using A only, cont in St st with double

seed-st edging until work measures 56¼in/143cm, ending

with RS facing for next row.

Work from ** to **.

Beg with a WS row, work 9 rows in St st with double seed-

st edging.

Work 12 rows in double seed st.

Bind off in patt.

Chart

Key

A: knit on RS, purl on WS

B: knit on RS, purl on WS

C: knit on RS, purl on WS

D: knit on RS, purl on WS

E: knit on RS, purl on WS

TWO-WAY VEST

YARN

7(8:9:10) x 1¾oz/153yd balls of Rowan *Kid Classic* in Tattoo 856

NEEDLES

Pair of size 7 (4.5mm) knitting needles

Pair of size 8 (5mm) knitting needles

Cable needle (CN)

GAUGE

23 sts and 25 rows to 4in/10cm over patt on size 8 (5mm) needles when lightly pressed *or size to obtain correct gauge.*

SPECIAL TECHNIQUES

Mid-row cast-on/bind-off, page 113

Cables, page 120

MEASUREMENTS

	S	M	L	XL	
Width	15	16	17	18	in
	38	41	43	46	cm
Length of fronts	19	21½	21½	24½	in
	48	55	55	62	cm

Please note that garment may drop in length during wear

SPECIAL ABBREVIATIONS

Tw2—knit into second st on left-hand needle, then knit first st and slip both sts off left-hand needle tog.

Cr4F—slip next st onto CN and hold at front of work, k3, then k1 from CN.

Cr4B—slip next 3 sts onto CN and hold at back of work, k1, then k3 from CN.

NOTE

Scarf is worked in one piece starting at right front.

SCARF

Using size 7 (4.5mm) needles, using the thumb method, cast on 117(117:138:138) sts.

Knit 3 rows.

Next row K4(4:6:6), [M1, k12(12:14:14)] 9 times, M1, k5(5:6:6). *127(127:148:148) sts.*

Place marker.

Change to size 8 (5mm) needles.

Row 1 (RS) K2, *row 1 of Chart A, p2, Tw2, p2, row 1 of Chart B, p2, Tw2, p2; rep from * 2(2:3:3) more times, row 1 of Chart A, p2, Tw2, p2, row 1 of Chart B, [row 1 Chart A] 1(1:0:0) time(s), k2.

Row 2 (WS) K2, [row 2 Chart A] 1(1:0:0) time(s), row 2 Chart B, k2, p2, k2, row 2 Chart A, *k2, p2, k2, row 2 Chart B, k2, p2, k2, row 2 Chart A; rep from * 2(2:3:3) more times, k2.

These 2 rows set g-st edges, chart placements, and dividing rev St st and twist patt.

Cont in 24-row rep as set on charts until work measures approx 19(21½:21½:24½)in/48(55:55:62)cm from marker, ending with row 22(18:16:12) patt and RS facing for next row.

** Shape armhole

Next row (RS) Patt 36, turn, and leave rem sts on a holder.

Working on these 36 sts only, work 4 rows, ending with WS facing for next row.

Leave these sts on a holder.

Rejoin yarn to rem sts, bind off 50(52:54:56), patt to end. *41(39:58:56) sts.*

Work 4 rows, ending with WS facing for next row.

Next row Patt 41(39:58:56), cast on 50(52:54:56) sts, work across 36 sts left on a holder. *127(127:148:148) sts.* **

Work 44(48:50:54) rows, ending with RS facing for next row.

Cont as foll:

Row 1 (RS) K2, *row 1 of Chart C, p2, Tw2, p2, row 1 of Chart D, p2, Tw2, p2; rep from * 2(2:3:3) more times, row 1 of Chart C, p2, Tw2, p2, row 1 of Chart D, [row 1 Chart C] 1(1:0:0) time(s), k2.

Row 2 (WS) K2, [row 2 Chart C] 1(1:0:0) time(s), row 2 Chart D, k2, p2, k2, row 2 Chart C, *k2, p2, k2, row 2 Chart D, k2, p2, k2, row 2 Chart C; rep from * 2(2:3:3) more times, k2.

These 2 rows set g-st edges, chart placements, and dividing rev St st and twist patt.

Work a further 42(46:48:52) rows, ending with RS facing for next row.

Work from ** to **.

Work to match right front to marker, ending with RS facing for next row.

Next row K4(4:6:6), [k2tog, k11(11:13:13)] 9 times, k2tog, k4(4:5:5). *117(117:138:138) sts.*

Knit 2 rows.

Bind off knitwise on WS.

Chart A

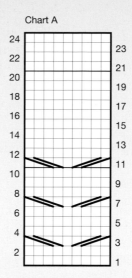

Chart B

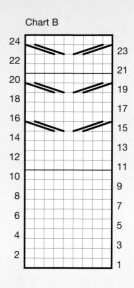

Chart C

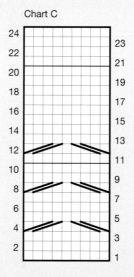

Chart D

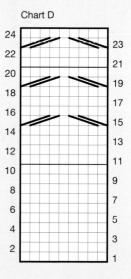

Key

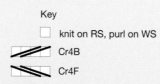

☐ knit on RS, purl on WS

▱ Cr4B

▱ Cr4F

CABLED WRAP

YARN

5(6:7:8:9) x 1¾oz/109yd balls of Rowan *Baby Alpaca DK* in Cheviot 207

GAUGE

22 sts and 30 rows to 4in/10cm over St st on size 6 (4mm) needles *or size to obtain correct gauge.*

NEEDLES

Pair of size 3 (3.25mm) knitting needles

Pair of size 6 (4mm) knitting needles

Cable needle (CN)

SPECIAL TECHNIQUES

Cables, page 120

MEASUREMENTS

	S	M	L	XL	XXL	
Width	17¾	19¾	22	24½	27	in
	45	50	56	62	69	cm
Length	15¾	15¾	19	19	19	in
	40	40	48	48	48	cm

SPECIAL ABBREVIATIONS

Cr5F—slip next st onto CN and hold at front of work, k4, then k1 from CN.

Cr3F—slip next st onto CN and hold at front of work, k2, then k1 from CN.

Cr5B—slip next 4 sts onto CN and hold at back of work, k1, then k4 from CN.

Cr3B—slip next 2 sts onto CN and hold at back of work, k1, then k2 from CN.

C2B—slip next st onto CN and hold at back of work, k1, then k1 from CN.

C2F—slip next st onto CN and hold and front of work, k1, then k1 from CN.

T2B—slip next st onto CN and hold at back of work, k1, then p1 from CN.

T2F—slip next st onto CN and hold at front of work, p1, then k1 from CN.

Wrap st—slip next st from left-hand needle onto right-hand needle, taking yarn to opposite side of work between the needles and then slipping the same st back onto left-hand needle. When working back across this st you may wish to pick up the wrapping loop with the wrapped st and work together.

NOTE

Wrap is worked in one piece starting at back hem.

WRAP

Using size 3 (3.25mm) needles, cast on
104(116:128:140:158) sts.

Row 1 (RS) K2, k1tbl, * p2, k1tbl, rep from * to last
2 sts, k2.

Row 2 K2, * p1, k2, rep from * to last 3 sts, p1, k2.

These 2 rows set rib and g-st edging.

Work 5 rows more in rib, ending with WS facing for next row.

Next row Patt 7, M1, patt 43(49:55:61:70), [M1,
patt 2] twice, M1, patt 43(49:55:61:70), M1, patt 7.
109(121:133:145:163) sts.

Change to size 6 (4mm) needles.

Row 1 K2, k1tbl, p2, k5, p2, k1tbl, p2, k10(16:22:28:37),
p2, k1tbl, work next 20 sts as set on row 1 of chart, k1tbl,
p2, k7, p2, k1tbl, work next 20 sts as set on row 1 of chart,
k1tbl, p2, k10(16:22:28:37), p2, k1tbl, p2, k5, p2, k1tbl, k2.

Row 2 K2, p1, k2, p5, k2, p1, k2, p10(16:22:28:37), k2,
p1, work next 20 sts as set on row 2 of chart, p1, k2, p7,
k2, p1, work next 20 sts as set on row 2 of chart, p1, k2,
p10(16:22:28:37), k2, p1, k2, p5, k2, p1, k2.

Row 3 K2, k1tbl, p2, k5, p2, k1tbl, p2, k10(16:22:28:37),
p2, k1tbl, work next 20 sts as set on row 3 of chart, k1tbl,
p2, k7, p2, k1tbl, work next 20 sts as set on row 3 of chart,
k1tbl, p2, k10(16:22:28:37), p2, k1tbl, p2, k5, p2, k1tbl, k2.

Row 4 K2, p1, k2, p5, k2, p1, k2, p10(16:22:28:37), k2,
p1, work next 20 sts as set on row 4 of chart, p1, k2, p7,
k2, p1, work next 20 sts as set on row 4 of chart, p1, k2,
p10(16:22:28:37), k2, p1, k2, p5, k2, p1, k2.

Row 5 K2, k1tbl, p2, Cr5F, p2, k1tbl, p2, k10(16:22:28:37),
p2, k1tbl, work next 20 sts as set on row 5 of chart, k1tbl,
p2, Cr3F, k1, Cr3B, p2, k1tbl, work next 20 sts as set on
row 5 of chart, k1tbl, p2, k10(16:22:28:37), p2, k1tbl, p2,
Cr5B, p2, k1tbl, k2.

Row 6 K2, p1, k2, p5, k2, p1, k2, p10(16:22:28:37), k2,
p1, work next 20 sts as set on row 6 of chart, p1, k2, p7,

k2, p1, work next 20 sts as set on row 6 of chart, p1, k2,
p10(16:22:28:37), k2, p1, k2, p5, k2, p1, k2.

These 6 rows set cables and set chart placement.

Cont in patt as set until work measures approx
15¾(15¾:19:19:19)in/40(40:48:48:48)cm, ending with row
6 of chart and RS facing for next row.

Place marker to denote length of back panel.

Next row Patt to last 11 sts, wrap next st, and turn.

Next row Patt to last 11 sts, wrap next st, and turn.

Next row Patt to last 14(15:16:17:19) sts, wrap next st,
and turn.

Next row Patt to last 14 (15:16:17:19) sts, wrap next st,
and turn.

Next row Patt to last 17(19:21:23:27) sts, wrap next st,
and turn.

Next row Patt to last 17(19:21:23:27) sts, wrap next st,
and turn.

Next row Patt to last 20 (23:26:29:35) sts, wrap next st,
and turn.

Next row Patt to last 20(23:26:29:35) sts, wrap next st,
and turn.

Next row Patt to last 23(27:31:35:43) sts, wrap next st,
and turn.

Next row Patt to last 23(27:31:35:43) sts, wrap next st,
and turn.

Next row Patt to last 26(31:36:41:51) sts, wrap next st,
and turn.

Next row Patt to end.

Split for front neck

Next row Patt 54(60:66:72:81), inc in next st, patt to end.
110(122:134:146:164) sts.

Next row Patt 54(60:66:72:81), inc in next st, turn and
leave rem sts on a holder. *56(62:68:74:83) sts.*

Working 2 sts at front edge in g st and all rem sts in patt,
cont in patt until work matches length of back panel

measured at side edge, ending with row 1 of patt and WS facing for next row.

Change to size 3 (3.25mm) needles.

Next row Patt 7, patt 2tog, patt 10, patt 2tog, patt 30(36:42:48:57), patt 2tog, patt 3. *53 (59:65:71:80) sts.*

Beg with row 1, work 7 rows in rib as set on back.

Bind off in rib.

Rejoin yarn to rem sts and cont in patt until work matches length of back panel measured at side edge, ending with

row 1 of patt and WS facing for next row.

Change to size 3 (3.25mm) needles.

Next row Patt 3, patt 2tog, patt 30(36:42:48:57), patt 2tog, patt 10, patt 2tog, patt 7. *53 (59:65:71:80) sts.*

Beg with row 1, work 7 rows in rib as set on back.

Bind off in rib.

FINISHING

Join side seams for approx 2in/5cm.

Key

□	knit on RS
●	purl on RS, knit on WS
႙	p1 tbl on WS
⫽	C2B
⧵⧵	C2F
⫽	T2B
⧵⧵	T2F

Chart

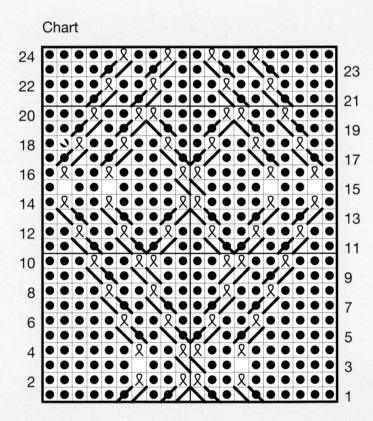

SIMPLE CORSAGE

FINISHED SIZE

4¾in/12cm diameter

YARN

1 x ⅞oz/229yd ball each of Rowan
Kidsilk Haze in:

A—Dewberry 600

B—Blackcurrant 641

Yarn used DOUBLE throughout

NOTIONS

Brooch finding

NEEDLES

Pair of size 6 (4mm) knitting needles

GAUGE

22 sts and 30 rows to 4in/10cm over
St st using yarn DOUBLE on size
6 (4mm) needles *or size to obtain
correct gauge.*

CENTER SECTION

Using yarn A DOUBLE, cast on 5 sts.

Row 1 Bind off 3 sts (1 st left on needle), k1.

Row 2 K2, cast on 3 sts.

Rep these 2 rows 3 times more.

Row 9 Bind off 3 sts (1 st left on needle), k1.

Row 10 K2, cast on 5 sts.

Row 11 Bind off 5 sts (1 st left on needle), k1.

Rep these 2 rows 8 times more.

Row 28 K2, cast on 8 sts.

Row 29 Bind off 8 sts (1 st left on needle), k1.

Rep these 2 rows 12 times more.

Change to yarn B and cont as foll:

Row 1 K2, cast on 10 sts.

Row 2 Bind off 10 sts (1 st left on needle), k1.

Rep these 2 rows 36 times more.

Bind off.

Bobbles (make 3)

Using yarn B DOUBLE, cast on 3 sts.

Row 1 K1, [k1, yo, k1] into next st, k1. *5 sts.*

Row 2 Purl.

Row 3 K1, sk2p, k1. *3 sts.*

Row 4 P3tog. Fasten off.

FINISHING

Sew center section together starting with the small "spikes" at the center and then spiralling the strip round, sewing in position at the same time. Run a gathering stitch around the edge of each bobble and pull to tighten. Sew bobbles in place on center section as shown. Attach brooch finding.

FRILLED SHAWL

FINISHED SIZE

Approx 46in/117cm at widest and
53cm/21in long

YARN

3 x 1¾oz/123yd balls of Rowan
Wool Cotton in Ship Shape 955 (A)
4 x ⅞oz/229yd balls of Rowan *Kidsilk
Haze* in Trance 582 (B)

NEEDLES

Pair of size 6 (4mm) knitting needles
Size 6 (4mm) circular needle—
change to circular needle when there
are too many sts for your straight
needle

GAUGE

22 sts and 30 rows to 4in/10cm over
patt on size 6 (4mm) needles *or size
to obtain correct gauge.*

SPECIAL TECHNIQUES

Provisional cast-on, page 112

SHAWL

Using a provisional cast-on (see page 112) and yarn A,
cast on 2 sts.

Knit 10 rows.

Turn work through 90 degrees and pick up 5 sts along
edge of this strip, then pull back provisional edging and
work across these 2 sts. *9 sts.*

Row 1 K1, inc in next st, knit to last 3 sts, inc in
next st, k2.

Row 2 K2, purl to last 2 sts, k2.

Rep these 2 rows once more. *13 sts.*

These 2 rows set shaping and g-st edging.

** Change to yarn B held DOUBLE.

Knit 2 rows.

Next row K2, * yo, k1, rep from * to last 2 sts, yo, k2. *23 sts.*

Knit 1 row. **

Change to yarn A.

Next row Knit.

Next row K2, purl to last 2 sts, k2.

These 2 rows set St st and g-st edgings.

Work 4 rows more in St st with g-st edging.

Work from ** to **. *43 sts.*

Change to yarn A and work 10 rows in St st with g-st
edging.

Work from ** to **. *83 sts.*

Change to yarn A and work 18 rows in St st with g-st
edging.

*** Change to yarn B held DOUBLE, knit 4 rows.

Next row K2, * yo, k1, rep from * to last 2 sts, yo, k2.
163 sts.

Knit 3 rows. ***

Change to yarn A and work 30 rows in St st with g-st
edging.

Work from *** to ***. *323 sts.*

Change to yarn A and work 30 rows in St st with g-st
edging.

Change to yarn B held DOUBLE.

Knit 4 rows.

Next row K2, * yo, k1, yo, k2tog, rep from * to last 3 sts, yo, k1, yo, k2. *431 sts.*

Knit 3 rows.

Leave these sts on the needle, ready for the edging.

Edging

Using yarn B held DOUBLE, cast on 15 sts.

Row 1 [K2tog, yo] 3 times, knit to last st of edging and k2tog with 1 st of main part.

Row 2 P14, k1.

Row 3 K1, [k2tog, yo] 3 times, knit to last st of edging and k2tog with 1 st of main part.

Row 4 As row 2.

Rep these 4 rows until all the sts of the main shawl have been used and only 15 sts rem.

Bind off.

Soak and block to size (see page 63).

SARAH SAYS

"I have worked this shawl in two different yarns in very similar colors but you could use a contrast yarn to make the eyelet bands and frilly edging really stand out. Once your shawl is finished, you will need to pin it out so that it is slightly stretched and a pleasing shape before covering with a damp cloth and leaving to dry."

COLLARED CAPE

YARN

3(3:4:4:5) x 1¾oz/191yd balls of
Rowan *Felted Tweed DK* in Clay 177

NEEDLES

Size 5 (3.75mm) circular needle
Size 3 (3.25mm) circular needle
Cable needle (CN)

NOTIONS

3 buttons, ½in/15mm diameter

GAUGE

23 sts and 32 rows to 4in/10cm over
St st on size 5 (3.75mm) circular
needle *or size to obtain correct
gauge.*

SPECIAL TECHNIQUES

Short-row shaping, page 114
Cables, page 120
No-turn bobbles, page 122

MEASUREMENTS

	S	M	L	XL	XXL	
Lower edge	45	50½	55½	61	66	in
	114	128	141	155	168	cm
Length	10½	12	12	13	13	in
	27	30	30	33	33	cm

SPECIAL ABBREVIATIONS

T3F—slip next 2 sts onto CN and hold at front of work, p1,
then k2 from CN.

T3B—slip next st onto CN and hold at back of work, k2,
then p1 from CN.

C3F—slip next 2 sts onto CN and hold at front of work, k1,
then k2 from CN.

C3B—slip next 2 sts onto CN and hold at back of work,
k2, then k1 from CN.

C5B—slip next 3 sts onto CN and hold at back of work,
k2, then p1, k2 from CN.

Wrap st—slip next st from left-hand needle onto right-
hand needle, taking yarn to opposite side of work between
the needles and then slipping the same st back onto left-

hand needle. When working back across this st you may
wish to pick up the wrapping loop with the wrapped st and
work together.

CAPE

Using size 5 (3.75mm) circular needle, cast on
275(307:339:371:403) sts.

Row 1 K1, p1, k1, * k2, [k1, p1] 4 times, k4, p1, k1, rep
from * to end.

Row 2 K1, p1, k1, * p2, [k1, p1] 4 times, k1, p2, k1, p1, k1,
rep from * to end.

These 2 rows set patt.

Work a further 12 rows in patt.

Next row K1, p1, k1, work 16-st rep as set of row 1 of

chart 17(19:21:23:25) times.

This row sets chart and seed st placement.

Cont in patt as set until all 27 rows have been completed, ending with WS facing for next row. *241(269:297:325:353) sts.*

Work 3 rows in seed st as set.

Beg with a K row, work 10(12:12:14:14) rows in St st.

Next row K3, * k4, sl2tog, k1, p2sso, k7, rep from * to end. *207(231:255:279:303) sts.*

Work 13(15:15:17:17) rows in St st without shaping.

Next row K3, * k3, sl2tog, k1, p2sso, k6, rep from * to end. *173(193:213:233:253) sts.*

Work 11(13:13:15:15) rows in St st without shaping.

Next row K3, * k2, sl2tog, k1, p2sso, k5, rep from * to end. *139(155:171:187:203) sts.*

Work 1 row, ending with RS facing for next row.

Shape front neck

Dec 1 st at each end of next and 4(3:3:2:2) foll alt rows, then on 0(1:1:2:2) foll 4th row(s). *129(145:161:177:193) sts.*

Work 1 row.

Next row Ssk, * k5, sl2tog, k1, p2sso, rep from * to last 7 sts, k5, k2tog. *97(109:121:133:145) sts.*

Work 5(7:7:9:9) rows, dec 1 st at each end of 2nd row and 0(0:2:3:3) foll alt rows. *95(107:115:125:137) sts.*

Bind off.

Collar

With RS facing, using size 3 (3.25mm) circular needle, pick up and knit 49(53:53:57:57) sts along front edge to start of neck shaping, 14(16:16:18:18) sts along neck shaping, 93(105:119:121:133) sts along bound-off edge, 14(16:16:18:18) sts down neck shaping and 49(53:53:57:57) sts along front edge. *219(243:257:271:283) sts.*

Row 1 (WS) K1, * p1, k1, rep from * to end.

This row sets seed st.

Work 3 rows more in seed st.

Next row Patt to last 47(51:51:55:55) sts, [bind off 2 sts (1 st left on needle), patt 6] twice, bind off 2 sts, patt to end.

Next row Patt to end, casting on 2 sts over gaps created by binding off on prev row.

Work 1 row.

Next row Patt 112(124:131:138:144), wrap next st, and turn.

Chart

Key

☐ knit on RS, purl on WS

● purl on RS, knit on WS

⅄ sk2p

Ⅴ (k1, yo, k1, yo, k1) into next stitch

▲ k1, sk2p, k1

5 k5 on RS, p5 on WS

3 k3 on RS, p3 on WS

C3B

C3F

T3B

T3F

C5B

Next row Patt 5, wrap next st, and turn,

Next row Patt 8, wrap next st, and turn,

Cont in this way working 3 sts more before wrapped st until the foll row has been completed:

Patt 110(122:134:140:152), wrap next st, and turn.

Next row Patt to end.

Work 1 row.

Next row Bind off 49(55:59:60:60) sts (1 st left on right-hand needle), pick up the loop between last and next st and work k1 into front, back, and front again of this loop, [slip these sts back onto left-hand needle, k3] 3 times, slip these sts back onto left-hand needle, sk2p, pass st left on right-hand needle over this st, **bind off 3 sts * rep from * to * 39(43:45:49:53) times in all, rep from * to ** once more, bind off rem sts.

FINISHING

Sew on buttons. Sew in ends and press lightly.

LOOPED SCARF

FINISHED SIZE

8¾ x 79in/22.5 x 200cm

YARN

5 x 1¾oz/109yd balls of Rowan *Lima*
in Lima 888

NEEDLES

Pair of size 9 (5.5mm) knitting
needles

GAUGE

20 sts and 26 rows to 4in/10cm over
St st using size 9 (5.5mm) needles *or
size to obtain correct gauge.*

SCARF

Cast on 45 sts.

Rows 1 and 2 Knit.

Row 3 (RS) K3, * p3, k3, rep from * to end.

Row 4 * P3, k3, rep from * to last 3 sts, p3.

Rows 5 and 6 As rows 3 and 4.

Row 7 As row 4.

Row 8 As row 3.

Rows 9 and 10 As rows 7 and 8.

The last 8 rows set block patt.

Rows 11 to 14 Rep rows 3 to 6. *(3 sets of blocks worked)*

Rows 15 to 20 Knit 6 rows.

Rows 21 to 48 Work rows 7 to 10, then rep rows 3 to 10
three times more. *(7 sets of blocks worked)*

Rows 49 to 52 Knit 4 rows.

These 52 rows set patt.

Cont in patt until work measures approx 79in/200cm in
block patt, ending with row 52.

Bind off. Join cast-on and bound-off edges to form a loop.

SARAH SAYS

"This pattern would make a great project for a
beginner to start understanding texture. Box
stitch is one of my favorites and is perfect for
this project as it looks good on both sides."

BEADED SCARF

FINISHED SIZE

5½ x 64¼in/14 x 164cm

YARN

3 x 1¾oz/123yd balls of Rowan
Wool Cotton in Bilberry 969

NEEDLES

Pair of size 6 (4mm) knitting needles

NOTIONS

Approx 800 beads, size 6

GAUGE

22 sts and 30 rows to 4in/10cm over
St st using size 6 (4mm) needles *or
size to obtain correct gauge.*

SPECIAL TECHNIQUES

Beading, page 129

SPECIAL ABBREVIATIONS

PB—Place bead by bringing yarn to front (RS) of work and
slipping the bead up next to st just worked, slip next st
purlwise from left needle to right needle before taking yarn
back to back (WS) of work, leaving bead sitting in front of
the slipped st on RS.

NOTE

Before starting to knit, thread beads onto yarn, see
page 129.

SCARF

Cast on 33 sts.

Row 1 (RS) K1, * PB, k1, rep from * to end.

Row 2 Purl.

Row 3 K1, * k1, PB, rep from * to last st 2 sts, k2.

Row 4 Purl.

Rep these 4 rows once more.

Cont as foll:

Row 1 [P1, k1] twice, work next 25 sts as set on row 1 of
chart, [k1, p1] twice.

Row 2 [P1, k1] twice, purl to last 3 sts, k1, p1, k1.

These 2 rows set seed-st edging and chart placement.

Cont as set until all 48 rows of chart have been completed,
ending with RS facing for next row.

Work rows 47 and 48 4 times more.

Work rows 43 to 48 once.

Rep last 14 rows twice more.

Work rows 47 and 48 4 times more.

Work rows 43 and 46 once.

Keeping edging as set throughout, beg with a K row,
working center 25 sts in St st, work 12 rows.

Work rows 47 and 48 as set on chart once.

Work rows 43 to 48 once.

Work rows 47 and 48 3 times.

Work rows 43 to 46 once.

Work 12 rows in St st on center sts.

Work rows 47 and 48 once.

Work rows 43 to 48 once.

Work rows 47 and 48 twice.

Work rows 43 to 46 once.

Work 12 rows in St st on center sts.

Work rows 47 and 48 once.

Work rows 43 to 48 once.

Work rows 47 and 48 once.

Work rows 43 to 46 once.

Cont in St st on center sts until scarf measures 15in/38cm from last beaded row.

Work rows 47 and 48 once.

Work rows 43 to 48 once.

Work rows 47 and 48 once.

Work rows 43 to 46 once.

Work 12 rows in St st on center sts.

Work rows 47 and 48 once.

Work rows 43 to 48 once.

Work rows 47 and 48 twice.

Work rows 43 to 46 once.

Work 12 rows in St st on center sts.

Work rows 47 and 48 as set on chart once.

Work rows 43 to 48 once.

Work rows 47 and 48 3 times.

Work rows 43 to 46 once.

Work 12 rows in St st on center sts.

Work rows 47 and 48 once.

** Work rows 43 to 48 once.

Work rows 47 and 48 4 times more. **

Work from ** to ** 3 times more.

Work rows 43 and 44 once more.

Work backward throughout chart from row 41 to 1.

Work 1 row, ending with RS facing for next row.

Row 1 (RS) K1, * PB, k1, rep from * to end.

Row 2 Purl.

Row 3 K1, * k1, PB, rep from * to last 2sts, k2.

Row 4 Purl.

Rep rows 1 to 3 once more.

Bind off knitwise on WS.

Chart

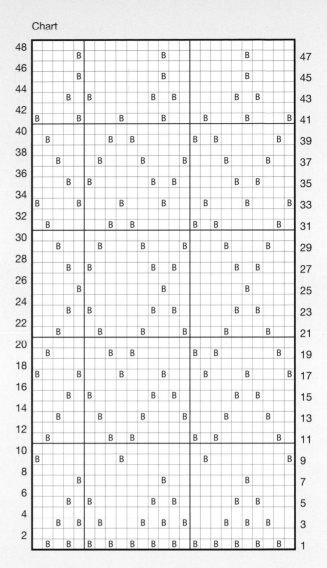

Key

knit on RS, purl on WS

B   PB

LACE BLOCK SHAWL

FINISHED SIZE

After light blocking approx 82in/208cm wide and 39½in/100cm deep

YARN

4 x ⅞oz/229yd balls of Rowan *Kidsilk Haze* in Trance 582

NEEDLES

Pair of size 5 (3.75mm) knitting needles

GAUGE

20 sts and 30 rows to 4in/10cm over patt on size 5 (3.75mm) needles *or size to obtain correct gauge.*

SPECIAL TECHNIQUES

Short-row shaping, page 114

Lace, page 124

SPECIAL ABBREVIATIONS

Wrap st—slip next st from left-hand needle onto right-hand needle, taking yarn to opposite side of work between the needles and then slipping the same st back onto left-hand needle. When working back across this st you may wish to pick up the wrapping loop with the wrapped st and work together.

NOTE

When working a lace pattern it is important to remember that if you are unable to work both the increase and corresponding decrease and vice versa, the stitches should be worked in stockinette stitch.

SHAWL

Panel A

Cast on 97 sts loosely.

Knit 4 rows.

Next row Knit.

Next row K2, purl to last 2 sts, k2.

These 2 rows set St st and g-st edgings.

Working in g st as set throughout and lace patt as set on Chart A, working 46-row rep 5 times, ending with RS facing for next row.

Knit 4 rows.

Shape panel A

Row 1 K2, yo, sk2p, yo, ssk, work sts 7 to 10 as set on row 1 of Chart B, beg with a first st work 10-st rep 8 times, k1, yo, sk2p, yo, k2.

Row 2 K2, purl to last 7 sts, p2tog tbl, p3, k2.

Row 3 K2, yo, sk2p, yo, ssk, work sts 9 and 10 as set on row 3 of Chart B, beg with a first st work 10-st rep 8 times, k1, yo, sk2p, yo, k2.

Rows 4, 6, 8, and 10 K2, purl to last 2 sts, k2.

Row 5 K2, yo, sk2p, yo, ssk, k1, beg with a first st work 10-st rep as set on row 5 of Chart B 8 times, k1, yo, sk2p, yo, k2.

Row 7 K2, yo, sk2p, yo, ssk, beg with a first st work 10-st rep as set on row 7 of Chart B 8 times, k1, yo, sk2p, yo, k2.

Row 9 K2, yo, sk2p, yo, ssk, work sts 2 to 10 as set on row 9 of Chart B once, then beg with first st work 10-st rep 7 times, k1, yo, sk2p, yo, k2.

Row 11 K2, yo, sk2p, yo, ssk, work sts 3 to 10 as set on row 9 of Chart B once, then beg with first st work 10-st rep 7 times, k1, yo, sk2p, yo, k2.

Row 12 K2, purl to last 2 sts, k2.

These 12 rows set decreases and chart placement.

** Working decreasing and lace patt as set, cont until 13 sts rem, ending with WS facing for next row.

Next row K2, p3, p3tog, p3, k2.

Next row K2, yo, ssk, sl2tog, k1, p2sso, k2tog, yo, k2.

Next row K2, p5, k2.

Next row K2, yo, sl2tog, k3tog, p2sso, yo, k2.

Next row K2, p3, k2.

Next row K2, sk2p, k2.

Next row K1, k3tog, k1.

Next row K3tog. Fasten off. **

Place a marker 19¾in/50cm up right side of panel from cast-on edge.

With RS facing, pick up and knit 97 sts between the cast-on edge and this marker.

Panel B

Knit 3 rows.

Work 2 rows in St st with g-st edging.

Working lace patt as set on Chart C, working 16-row rep 5 times, ending with RS facing for next row.

Knit 4 rows.

Shape panel B

Row 1 (RS) K2, yo, sk2p, yo, k1, beg with first st work 10-st rep set on row 1 of Chart D 8 times, work sts 1 to 4 once more, k2tog, yo, sk2p, yo, k2.

Row 2 K2, p3, p2tog, purl to last 2 sts, k2.

Row 3 K2, yo, sk2p, yo, k1, beg with first st work 10-st rep as set on row 3 of Chart D 8 times, work sts 1 and 2 once more, k2tog, yo, sk2p, yo, k2.

Rows 4, 6, 8, and 10 K2, purl to last 2 sts, k2.

Row 5 K2, yo, sk2p, yo, k1, beg with first st work as set on row 5 of Chart D to last 7 sts, k2tog, yo, sk2p, yo, k2.

Row 7 K2, yo, sk2p, yo, k1, beg with first st work as set on row 7 of Chart D to last 7 sts, k2tog, yo, sk2p, yo, k2.

Row 9 K2, yo, sk2p, yo, k1, beg with first st work as set on row 9 of Chart D 7 times, work sts 1 to 9 once more, k2tog, yo, sk2p, yo, k2.

Row 11 K2, yo, sk2p, yo, k1, beg with first st work as set on row 11 of Chart D 7 times, work sts 1 to 8 once more, k2tog, yo, sk2p, yo, k2.

Row 12 K2, purl to last 2 sts, k2.

These 12 rows set decreases and chart placement.

Work from ** to ** as set on Panel A.

Panel C

With RS facing, pick up and knit 60 sts down straight side of Panel B, pick up 1 st from center point where Panel A and B meet, pick up and knit 60 sts up straight side of Panel A. *121 sts.*

Place a marker after 59th st.

Row 1 and every foll alt row (WS) K2, purl to last 2 sts, k2.

Row 2 K2, [k2, k2tog, yo, k2tog, yo, k1] 7 times, k2, [k2tog, yo] twice, k1, k2tog, k1, ssk, k1, [yo, ssk] twice, k2, [k1, yo, ssk, yo, ssk, k2] 7 times, k2.

Row 4 K2, [k1, k2tog, yo, k2tog, yo, k2] 7 times, k1, [k2tog, yo] twice, k1, k2tog, k1, ssk, k1, [yo, ssk] twice, k1, [k2, yo, ssk, yo, ssk, k1] 7 times, k2.

Row 6 K2, [k2tog, yo, k2tog, yo, k3] 7 times, [k2tog, yo] twice,k1, k2tog, k1, ssk, k1, [yo, ssk] twice, [k3, yo, ssk, yo, ssk] 7 times, k2.

Row 8 K3, k2tog, yo, [k3, k2tog, yo, k2tog, yo] 7 times, k1, k2tog, k1, ssk, k1, [yo, ssk, yo, ssk, k3] 7 times, yo, ssk, k3.

Row 10 K2, k2tog, yo, [k3, k2tog, yo, k2tog, yo] 7 times, k1, k2tog, k1, ssk, k1, [yo, ssk, yo, ssk, k3] 7 times, yo, ssk, k2. *111 sts*.

Row 11 K2, purl to last 2 sts, k2.

Cont as foll:

Row 1 (RS) K58, wrap next st, turn.

Row 2 P2togtbl, p3, wrap next st, turn.

Row 3 K2tog, K4, wrap next st, turn.

Row 4 P7, wrap next st, turn.

Row 5 K9, wrap next st, turn.

Row 6 P2tog, p9, wrap next st, turn.

Row 7 K2tog, k10, wrap next st, turn.

Row 8 P13, wrap next st, turn.

Row 9 K15, wrap next st, turn.

Row 10 P2tog, p15, wrap next st, turn.

Row 11 K2tog, k16, wrap next st, turn.

Row 12 P19, wrap next st, turn.

Row 13 K21, wrap next st, turn.

Row 14 P2tog, p21, wrap next st, turn.

Row 15 K2tog, k22, wrap next st, turn.

Row 16 P25, wrap next st, turn.

Row 17 K11, work next 3 sts as set on row 1 of Chart E, k13, wrap next st, turn.

Row 18 P2tog, p27, wrap next st, turn.

Row 19 K2tog, k10, work next 5 sts as set on row 3 of Chart E, k13, wrap next st, turn.

Row 20 P31, wrap next st, turn.

Row 21 K12, work next 7 sts as set on row 5 of Chart E, k14, wrap next st, turn.

Row 22 P2tog, p33, wrap next st, turn.

Row 23 K2tog, k4, work next 25 sts as set on row 7 of Chart E, k5, wrap next st, turn.

Row 24 P37, wrap next st, turn.

Row 25 K6, work next 27 sts as set on row 9 of Chart E, k6, wrap next st, turn.

Row 26 P2tog, p39, wrap next st, turn.

Row 27 K2tog, k5, work next 29 sts as set on row 11 of Chart E, k6, wrap next st, turn.

Row 28 P43, wrap next st, turn.

Row 29 K8, work next 29 sts as set on row 13 of Chart E, k8, wrap next st, turn.

Row 30 P2tog, p45, wrap next st, turn.

Row 31 K2tog, k8, work next 29 sts as set on row 15 of Chart E, k9, wrap next st, turn.

Row 32 P49, wrap next st, turn.

Row 33 K11, work next 29 sts as set on row 17 of Chart E, k11.

Row 34 P2tog, p51, wrap next st, turn.

Row 35 K2tog, k11, work next 29 sts as set on row 19 of Chart E, k12.

Row 36 P56, wrap next st, turn.

Row 37 K14, work next 29 sts as set on row 21 of Chart E, k14, wrap next st, turn.

Row 38 P2tog, p57, wrap next st, turn.

Row 39 K2tog, k58, wrap next st, turn.

Row 40 P61, wrap next st, turn.

Row 41 K64, wrap next st, turn.

Row 42 P2tog, p66, wrap next st, turn.

Row 43 K2tog, k70, wrap next st, turn.

Row 44 P76, wrap next st, turn.

Row 45 K79, k2tog, wrap next st, turn.

Row 46 Purl to last 2 sts, p2tog.

Cont as foll:

Next row K1, k2tog, turn.

Next row K2.

Rep these 2 rows until only 4 sts rem.

Next row [K2tog] twice.

Next row K2tog and fasten off.

Soak and block to size (see page 63).

Chart A

Key
□ knit on RS, purl on WS
● purl on RS, knit on WS
╱ ssk
╲ k2tog
⅄ sk2p
○ yo

93

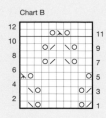

Chart B

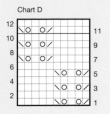

Chart D

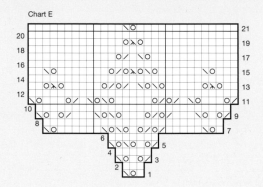

Chart E

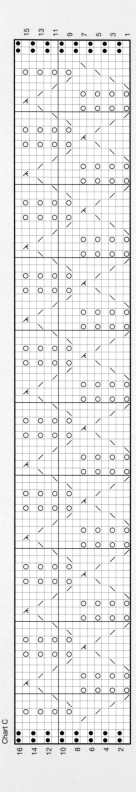

Chart C

Key

☐ knit on RS, purl on WS

● purl on RS, knit on WS

◥ ssk

◢ k2tog

⅄ sk2p

○ yo

94

ABBREVIATIONS

The knitting pattern abbreviations used in this book are as below:

alt	alternate
approx	approximate
beg	begin(s)(ning)
cm	centimeters
CN	cable needle
cont	continu(e)(ing)
dec	decreas(e)(ing)
DPN	double-pointed needles
foll	follow(s)(ing)
g st	garter stitch (K every row)
in	inch(es)
inc	increas(e)(ing)
K	knit
K2tog	knit next 2 stitches together
m	meter(s)
M1	make one stitch by picking up horizontal loop before next stitch and knitting into back of it
mm	millimeters
P	purl
patt	pattern
psso	pass slipped stitch over
p2sso	pass two slipped stitches over
P2tog	purl next 2 stitches together
rem	remain(s)(ing)
rep	repeat
rev St st	reverse stockinette stitch
RS	right side
skp	sl 1, k1, psso
sk2p	sl 1, k2tog, psso
sl 1	slip one stitch
sl2tog	slip 2 stitches together
ssk	slip, slip, knit
st(s)	stitch(es)
St st	stockinette stitch (1 row K, 1 row P)
tbl	through back of loop(s)
tog	together
WS	wrong side
yd	yard(s)
yo	yarn over right needle to make a new stitch

HOW TO WEAR

Many of the designs in the gallery section of this book (see pages 8–49) are very versatile. You can wear them in so many different ways, creating a wide range of special looks, dressed up or down. These include ways to wrap, fasten, belt, or tie the scarves, depending on the style of the project and the form of the design, plus inherent versatility within the design itself. This chapter also offers practical information on how to tie some attractive knot styles.

LONG NARROW SCARVES

Here are some different ways to wear a scarf. These styles are great with longer, thinner scarves. Shown here with the Chevron scarf (see pattern, page 55).

1 OVER THE SHOULDER

Loop the scarf around your neck in the usual way, with one long end at the front and the other over your shoulder, at the back.

2 LOOPED THROUGH

Fold the scarf in half lengthwise. Place it around the back of your neck with the folded end to one side and the doubled ends to the other. Feed the ends of the scarf through the loop and pull to tighten loosely.

3 HALF LOOP

Loop the scarf around your neck in the usual way, tie the two ends then bring one length back through the loop and fold over the tie so that it sits with a soft fold at the front.

1

2

3

WIDER SCARVES AND STOLES

Here are some ways that particularly suit a wide scarf or stole. Shown here with the Fairisle stole (see pattern, page 74).

1 BASIC KNOT
Loop the scarf around your neck and then make a simple fold-over knot.

2 PINNED WITH A BROOCH
Throw one end of the scarf over one shoulder and pin in place with a large brooch.

3 BELTED
Place the scarf around your neck with the ends hanging equally on either side. Belt it in at the waist to form a wrap.

1

2

3

MULTIFUNCTIONAL DESIGN

This design for the Multiway stole was planned with different ways to wear it, with buttons as part of the design—see Diagram 1 on page 57 (see pattern, page 56).

1 LOOSE
Here, the scarf is unbuttoned and shown laying flat, simply draped around the neck.

2 SHRUG
Button together A and C, then do the same with B and D. These now form "sleeves" so you can wear it as a shrug.

3 CAPE
Drape the stole over your shoulders to cover them and button A and B at the front.

4 PONCHO
Fasten A and B at the front of your body, along with as many buttons of C and D as you need to create a comfortable fit.

5 BOLERO
Wrap the stole "every which way" around your neck and fasten a few buttons to hold it in position.

1

2

3

4

5

TYING SPECIAL KNOTS 1

This knot style works particularly well with more glamorous scarves and shawls. Shown here with the Lace block shawl (see pattern, page 90).

1 *Place the shawl around your shoulders, then cross the ends of the shawl at the front.*

2 *Take the length which sits on top and wrap it over and back under the other length.*

3 *Repeat step 2 so you are left with the end of the shawl wrapped twice.*

4 *Take the wrapping end behind and up through the loop around your neck and then down through the second wrapping loop and tighten.*

1

2

3

4

TYING SPECIAL KNOTS 2

This fancy knot works really well for longer, thinner scarves. Shown here with the Bold stripe scarf (see pattern, page 54).

1 Fold the scarf in half lengthwise and place it around the back of your neck.

2 Feed one end of the scarf through the folded loop on the other side of your neck.

3 Create a twist in the loop end of the scarf, just below the end you have fed through.

4 Now feed the second end of the scarf through this lower loop, pull gently to tighten, and arrange neatly.

1

2

3

4

TYING SPECIAL KNOTS 3

This works well with fine or glamorous scarves that roll well. Shown here with the Beaded scarf (see pattern, page 88).

1 *Leaving the center of the scarf at the front neck, cross the two ends at the back.*

2 *Bring one end of the scarf back to the front and down through the loop.*

3 *Repeat step 2 with the other end, then tighten and arrange as necessary.*

1

2

3

SPECIAL TECHNIQUES

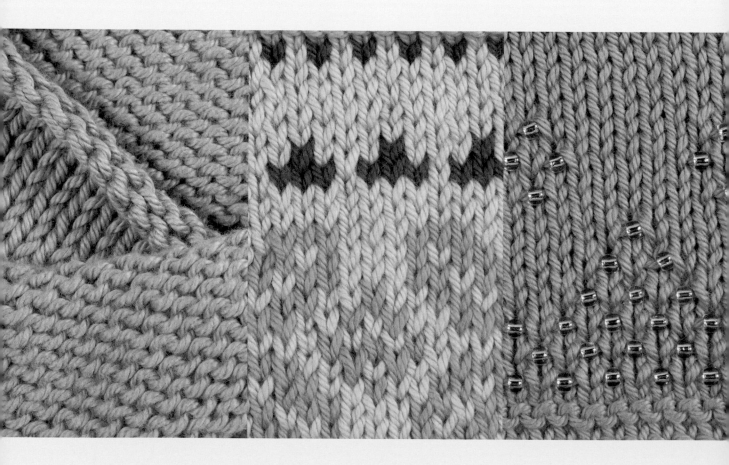

The following techniques serve as further explanation to those used in the pattern pages (see pages 50–94) of this book. They include a wide range, from special ways to cast on and bind off to particular shaping techniques, and they also include some more general techniques: for example how to create textural stitches, such as cables and lace, and how to knit with beads.

PROVISIONAL CAST-ON

This technique allows you to cast on without having a firm edge. When you unpick the spare yarn, the stitches appear open which allows you to then pick them up and work an edging of your choice, which will give you a seamless join.

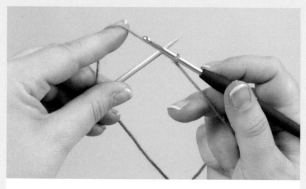

1 Using a crochet hook and one knitting needle, make a slip knot and place onto the crochet hook. Holding the yarn in your left hand, place the knitting needle over the yarn.

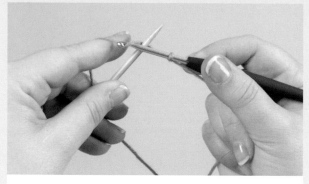

2 Place the crochet hook under the yarn and bring through the slip knot on the hook. As you pull through the slip knot a loop will form over the knitting needle.

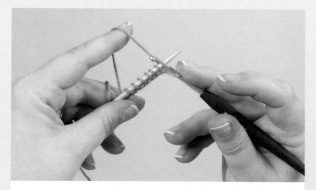

3 Repeat until you have the required amount of stitches. Once you have the required amount, thread yarn through last crochet chain.

4 Join in the main yarn for the garment and knit into stitches on the knitting needle. When piece is complete and you are ready to pick up the cast-on edge, simply unpick the crochet edge.

MID-ROW CAST-ON/ BIND-OFF

This useful technique is used for, among other things, buttonholes and pockets. In this book it is used to create the armholes in the Two-way vest (see page 76). Pay attention to the final step, which helps to create a neater hole than if you cast on in the normal way.

1 Work to the point where the hole is required. Bind off the required number of stitches before continuing to the end of the row.

2 Work back to the point where the stitches were bound off, turn, and cast on using the cable technique (see page 120).

3 When you get to the last cast-on stitch, before placing the stitch onto the left-hand needle, bring the yarn to the front between the needles.

4 Knit in the normal way across the remaining stitches.

SHORT-ROW SHAPING

This technique allows you to shape the work in such a way that it leaves no unsightly holes and can be used for shaping a shoulder, to create a flared hem, or to make an entire shaped piece of knitting, such as the Crescent shawl on page 62.

The technique involves wrapping the yarn around the stitch, which leaves a loop at the front of the work. This is picked up and knitted into the adjoining stitch as you work back. This is referred to in the pattern with the term Wrap st.

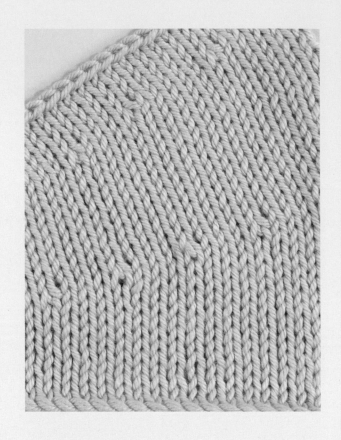

1 Knit along the row to the point where you need to Wrap st. Bring yarn forward between the needles.

2 Slip the next stitch from the left-hand needle onto the right-hand needle.

3 Take yarn back between the needles to the back of the work. Turn and work back across the row in pattern.

4 When short-row shaping has been completed you will be left with the wrapped stitch sitting at the front of the work.

5 Once all the shaping is completed, knit a complete row, picking up the loop of the wrapped stitch with the point of your right-hand needle.

6 Knit this loop together with the next stitch on the left-handle needle.

7 Continue and repeat across all of the wrapped stitches.

8 You can see here that the slope is neat and tidy.

MOBIUS SHAPING

This technique, popularly known as mobius knitting or mobius cast-on, creates an interesting twist in the shape of knitting worked in the round.

There are several ways to create this twist, but the one shown in the scarf on page 67 is done by the method shown here. In it, you start by casting on in the way shown, transferring half of the stitches to the other end of the needle, so that your circular needle develops a twist, which translates into a twist in the knitting.

To work this method for the scarf in this book, you need a 40-in/100-cm long circular needle.

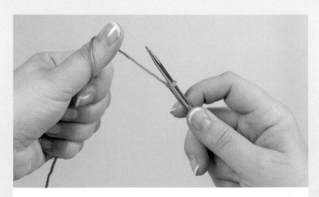

1 Make a slip knot and place it on the point of your circular needle, then wrap the ball yarn around the thumb from front to back.

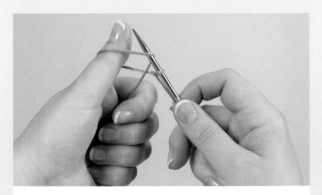

2 Insert the point of the needle under the yarn across the front of the thumb and then pull the yarn tight, slipping it off the thumb onto the needle.

3 Repeat steps 1 and 2 until you have the desired number of stitches (half of the total number given in the mobius scarf pattern).

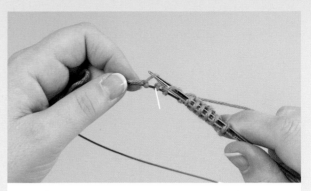

4 Now push the stitches onto the wire of the needle. Using the other point of the circular needle, pick up the loop that lies between the first two stitches.

5 Knit into this loop and continue to pick up and knit each loop until you reach the slip knot where you began.

6 Knit into the slip knot and place a colored yarn marker.

7 Now knit into the first stitch of the left-hand point of the circular needle. Continue to knit across all the stitches.

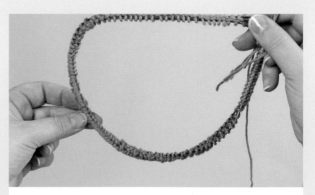

8 Your circular needle will have developed a twist (translating into a twist in your knitting). The stitches may feel a bit tight until you have worked a few rows, but it will work!

KNITTED-ON EDGING

Using this technique you can work a decorative edging to your knitting while binding off at the same time. The benefit is that this creates a neater, looser edge than a sewn-on one, which helps your scarf or shawl to drape beautifully. It is shown here with a garter-stitch edging, but can be worked in whatever stitch is required.

The cast-on method used here is the two-needle method, also known as Cable cast-on, which produces a neat, firm edge.

Cable cast-on

1 Cast on the required number of stitches for the added edging by placing the needle between the first and second stitches on your left-hand needle.

2 Wrap the yarn round the point of the right-hand needle and bring through to create a loop.

3 Slip the loop on the left-hand needle and repeat until the required number of stitches for the edging are on the left-hand needle.

Knitting the edging

1 Knit across the stitches of your edging until one stitch of the edging is left to be worked.

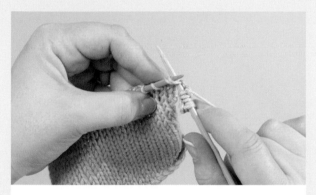

2 Knit this stitch together with the first stitch of the main part of the work. Turn.

3 Now work back across the stitches of the edging, in pattern. Turn.

4 Work to the last stitch of the border, then knit this together with the first stitch of the main piece of the work.

5 Continue, so that the edging is knitted while the stitches of the main piece of the work are bound off.

CABLES

Cabling is the technique that allows you to move a number of stitches across to another part of the row. You do this by holding the relevant number of stitches on a special cable needle. The use of a special cable needle and the twists in the cabled stitches make it look harder than it is.

Cables can be created over different numbers of stitches to create differing sized patterns. The actual number of stitches to be cabled is given in the special note with each cable pattern.

The cable pattern instruction is abbreviated as C (for cable), 6 (or other number of stitches), then F (for forward cable) or B (for back cable). The technique is the same regardless of the number of stitches.

Reversible cable

The example (above) shows a six-stitch cable worked in k1, p1 rib, so the cable is reversible. It is ideal on a scarf or wrap where the wrong side will easily be seen.

Cable six-stitch forward (C6F)

1 Work to position on the needle where the cable has to be worked. Slip 3 (or required number of stitches) onto the cable needle.

2 Holding the cable needle at the front of the work, work 3 stitches from your normal left-hand needle.

3 Keeping your normal left-hand needle to the back, work the 3 stitches from the cable needle.

4 Put down your cable needle. Continue to work across the row. You can see how the stitches have been crossed and the cable is traveling to the left.

Cable six-stitch back (C6B)

1 To cross the cable back, work across the row to the position of the cable and slip the next 3 stitches onto the cable needle.

2 Hold the cable needle at the back of the work and work 3 stitches from your normal left-hand needle.

3 Now work the 3 stitches from the cable needle.

4 Put down the cable needle. Continue to work across the row. You can see how the stitches have been crossed and the cable is traveling to the right.

NO-TURN BOBBLES

Knitted bobbles give texture and are traditionally used in Aran designs. Bobbles are usually worked in stockinette stitch on a reverse stockinette stitch background so that they stand out.

There are various sizes of bobble and several different methods of making them. We have chosen to demonstrate a method where you don't need to keep turning the work.

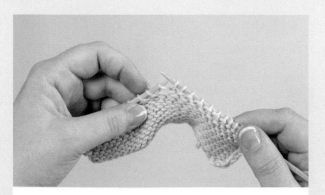

1 Work to the position of the required bobble. Knit into the front stitch without removing the loop from the left-hand needle.

2 Still with the loop on the left-handle needle, now work into the back of the same stitch.

3 Repeat steps 1 and 2, working first into the front and then into the back of the stitch three more times.

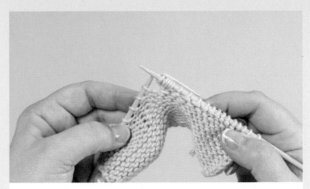

4 You should now have 5 stitches (which will form your first bobble) on the right-hand needle.

5 Slip these 5 stitches back onto the left-hand needle.

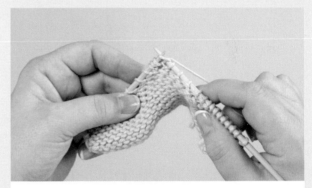

6 Now knit these 5 stitches by bringing the yarn tight round the back of these 5 stitches.

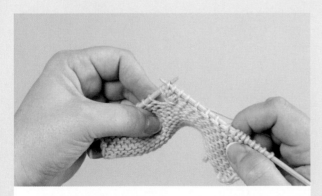

7 When all 5 stitches are knitted, slip them back onto the left-hand needle and repeat step 6 two more times.

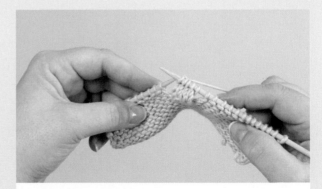

8 Slip all 5 stitches onto the left-hand needle and knit 2 together twice, knit the last stitch, slip back onto the left-hand needle, and knit all 3 stitches together to complete the bobble.

LACE

Lace knitting is worked as a series of loops and eyelets to create an open, lightweight fabric. In most cases, this is created by bringing the yarn forward over the needle and working a corresponding decrease to keep the stitch count even. When bringing the yarn forward to create a loop, it is described in various ways (yo, yfwd, or yon) according to the stitch pattern, but in this book the only yarn forward used is the one known as yo.

When decreasing, different techniques are employed to slope stitches to the left or the right. To create a left-slope decrease, follow the skp instruction. To make a right-slope decrease, follow the ssk instruction.

Yarn over (yo)

1 To make a decorative hole in the work, bring the yarn to the front of the work between the two needles.

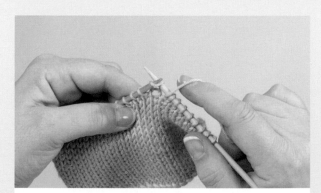

2 According to the pattern, either slip or knit the next stitch in the usual way, taking the yarn across the right-hand needle.

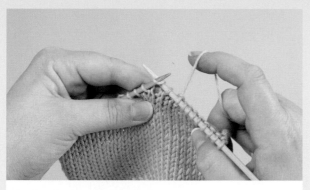

Left-slope decrease (skp)

1 To work this decrease, slip the first stitch and knit the next stitch...

2 ... then pass the slipped stitch over the knitted stitch.

Right-slope decrease (ssk)

1 Slip the next two stitches onto the right-hand needle...

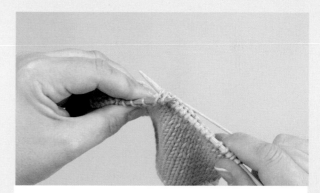

2 ... and insert the left-hand needle into the front of both these stitches.

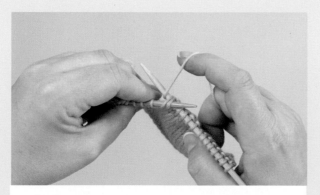

3 Now knit the two stitches together. This will allow the stitches to slope to the right.

FAIRISLE: TWO-HANDED

Fairisle is the traditional Scottish method of working more than one color repeatedly in a row, with the color not being worked stranded across the back of the work.

When working with two or more colors in a row, it is important to make sure that the yarns do not tangle (the two-handed method shown here helps to avoid this) and it is also important that you change yarns consistently each time, as shown in steps 4–7, to avoid creating holes and to ensure that the stranded yarns (ie the yarns not in use) are neatly woven on the back of the work.

If there are more than three consecutive stitches of one color in a row, you will need to catch the stranded yarn at the back of the work (see page 128) to prevent large loops forming.

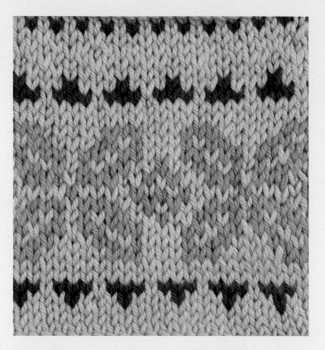

NOTE The steps here demonstrate the two-color Fairisle technique using two hands. The left hand technique picks the yarn up with the needle (Continental style). The right hand loops the yarn over the needle (English style).

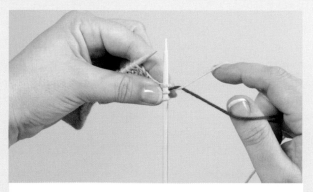

Joining in new yarn
Join in the new (second) yarn by twisting the yarns together at the back of the work and knit one stitch in the new contrasting yarn.

Knit row (two hands)
1 Holding new color over your left forefinger and first color over your right, insert the tip of the needle into the stitch to be worked and take it OVER the new yarn.

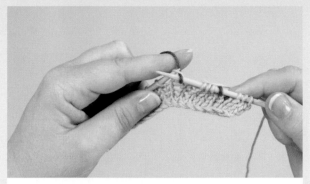

2 Pick up the new yarn with the needle, drawing it through the stitch on the needle to make the next stitch.

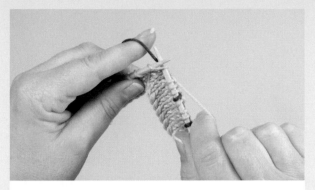

3 Knit along the rest of the row, knitting the first color with your right hand and knitting the new color with your left, as in steps 1 and 2.

Purl row (two hands)

4 Work the first stitch of the purl row, then bring the new yarn under the first yarn, holding it over forefinger of right hand. This prevents a hole forming.

5 Each time you change color, keeping one yarn in the right hand and the other under the thumb of the left hand, as the needle goes into the first stitch take it UNDER the left-hand yarn.

6 Then draw the needle and yarn through the loop to knit the stitch.

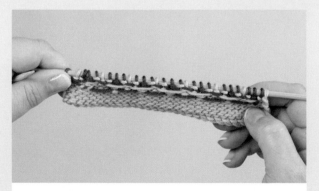

7 Repeat these steps each time you change color, so both yarns are stranded evenly and neatly across the back of the work without pulling or puckering.

FAIRISLE: CARRYING YARNS

When you knit three or more stitches of any color in a Fairisle row, it helps to prevent the non-working yarns looping at the back of the work if you catch them invisibly as you knit (without pulling them through to the right side). Hold the yarns in both hands as on the previous pages.

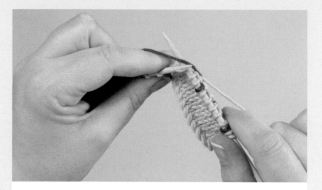

Knit row

1 Knit two stitches, then insert the needle into the next stitch taking it under the left-hand yarn.

2 Knit the stitch in the usual way making sure that you hold the other yarn up on the left forefinger so you do not pull it through the stitch you are knitting.

Purl row

1 To catch the yarn on a purl row, purl two stitches then insert the needle into the stitch to be worked, under the other yarn.

2 Work the next stitch, keeping the other yarn held up high so that it doesn't get pulled through with the stitch you are working.

BEADING

Adding beads to your knitting gives the finished pieces a luxurious touch. You can use beads sparingly, to highlight an edging, or as an all-over patterning decorative device. The beads need to be threaded onto the yarn before you knit, so you need to count the beads carefully. As they form an integral part of the knitted piece, they should ideally be made of glass and washable.

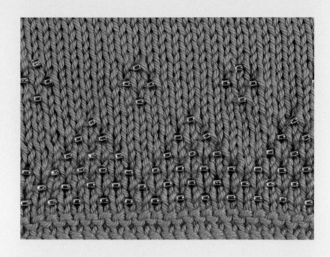

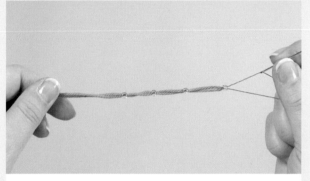

Threading the beads

Thread a sewing needle with cotton thread, loop it and tie a knot. Pass yarn through loop, and pass the bead over the needle and thread onto yarn.

Knitting with beads

1 Knit to the position where the first bead needs to be incorporated and bring the yarn forward.

2 Now slip the next stitch purlwise.

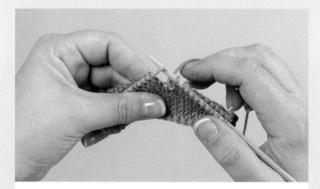

3 Slip the bead down the yarn until it is at the front of the work and then bring the yarn between the needles to the back of the work, before knitting the next stitch firmly.

PICKING UP STITCHES FOR EDGINGS

When picking up stitches for an edging, you do not necessarily pick up every stitch from the cast-on or bound-off edge of the main piece. However, you need to pick up stitches evenly and without adding bulk behind the pick-up row. If you are picking up a large number of stitches, section the work from which you are picking up the stitches and then pick up every third stitch and then every second stitch, alternately, to spread any bulk.

It is also best NOT to slip the first stitch of a row. Make sure you knit a stitch on a knit row and purl it on a purl row to avoid a bobbly edge behind the picked up stitches.

1 Divide the edge of the work where the stitches are being picked up into even sections, marking them with a pin. Start by marking the halfway point and then divide evenly again, as needed.

2 Look at the stitches along the edge to be picked up from. Each stitch forms a "V" shape (the needle points to one of them).

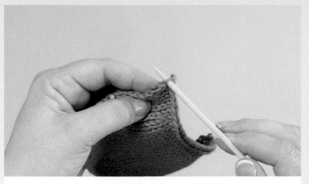

3 Insert the needle into the arm of the "V," always the nearest one facing you.

4 Then loop the yarn around the needle and bring it through the stitch to knit it.

5 Continue to work along the edge, picking up and knitting 2 more consecutive stitches (3 in total).

6 Now miss the next stitch before knitting 2 more consecutive stitches.

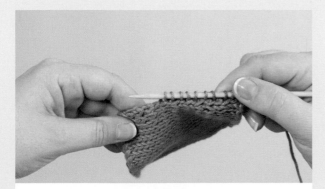

7 Continue along the edge, repeating steps 5 and 6 to pick up and knit 3 stitches, miss one, pick up and knit 2 stitches, until you have worked along the whole row.

8 At the end of the row, you will have picked up all the stitches. If you have picked up carefully, using the same side of each "V," the stitches next to the picked up stitches look unbroken.

USEFUL INFORMATION

SIZING

The instructions are given for the smallest size, and larger sizes follow in parentheses. If there is only one set of figures, it refers to all sizes. If - (hyphen) or 0 (zero) is given in an instruction for the size you are knitting, then that particular instruction does not apply to your size.

GAUGE

This controls both the shape and size of an article, so any variation, however slight, can distort the finished garment. Although the patterns in this book are not mostly fitted, if you want to achieve the sizes given, you must match the gauge given at the start of each pattern. To check your gauge, knit a square in the pattern stitch and/or stockinette stitch of perhaps 5–10 more stitches and 5–10 more rows than those given in the gauge note. Press the finished square under a damp cloth and mark out the central 4in/10cm square with pins. If you have too many stitches to 4in/10cm, try again using thicker needles. If you have too few stitches to 4in/10cm, try again using finer needles. Once you have achieved the correct gauge, your garment will be knitted to the right size.

Chart notes

Many patterns in this book are worked from charts. Each square of the chart represents a stitch and each line of squares represents a row of knitting. Where the chart is for colorwork, each color used is given a different letter in a key shown alongside the chart and these letters are shown too in the list of yarns used in each pattern. Where the chart demonstrates a special stitch or bead, the key in the chart refers to the instruction in the pattern. When working from charts, read odd-numbered rows (K) from right to left and even-numbered rows (P) from left to right, unless otherwise stated.

Cable patterns

Cable stitch patterns allow you to twist the stitches in various ways, to create an interesting ropelike structure to the knitting.The cables can be just a couple of stitches wide or really big and chunky (up to 8 stitches or more). You need to hold the appropriate number of stitches that form the cable twist (written in the pattern with the abbreviation CN) on a separate small cable needle, while you knit behind them or in front of them. You then knit the stitches off the cable needle before continuing to knit the remaining stitches in the row.

Depending on whether the cable needle is at the front or the back of the work, the cables will twist to the left or the right (for example, CN4F) or to the back (for example, CN4B) but the principle remains the same. See Cables, page 120.

Fairisle

Fairisle is the name given to working two or more colors in a single row of knitting, taking the yarn not in use across the back of the knitting. It requires a special technique (see pages 126–128).

FINISHING METHODS

Blocking and pressing

Block out each piece of knitting by pinning it on a board to the correct measurements in the pattern. Cover with damp cloths and leave to dry. Then lightly press it according to the ball band instructions, omitting any ribbed areas. For lace items, see blocking instructions on page 63.

Take special care to press the edges as this makes sewing up easier and neater. If you cannot press the fabric, then cover the knitted fabric with a damp cloth and allow it to stand for a couple of hours. Darn in all ends neatly along the selvedge edge or a color join, as appropriate.

Stitching seams

When you stitch the pieces together, remember to match any areas of color and texture carefully where they meet. Use a special seam stitch, called mattress stitch, as it creates the neatest flattest seam. After all the seams are complete, press the seams and hems. Lastly, sew on the buttons to correspond with the positions of the buttonholes.

For a list of knitting abbreviations used in the patterns, see page 95.

ROWAN YARN INFORMATION

All the projects in this book are knitted in Rowan yarns and the entries below give the Rowan information supplied with the yarn.

Baby Alpaca DK

A 100 percent baby alpaca yarn; 1¾oz/50g (109yd/100m) per ball; 22 sts and 30 rows to 4in/10cm in St st using size 6 (4mm) knitting needles.

Felted Tweed DK

A wool-alpaca-viscose mix; 50 percent merino wool, 25 percent alpaca wool, 25 percent viscose; 1¾oz/50g (191yd/175m) per ball; 22–24 sts and 30–32 rows to 4in/10cm in St st using size 5–6 (3.25–4mm) knitting needles.

Fine Lace

A baby alpaca (80 percent), merino wool (20 percent) mix yarn; 1¾oz/50g (436yd/400m) per ball; 20–39 sts and 35–45 rows to 4in/10cm in St st using size 0–6 (2–4mm) knitting needles.

Kid Classic

A lambswool-mohair-polyamide mix yarn (70 percent lambswool, 25 percent kid mohair, 4 percent polyamide); 1¾oz/50g (153yd/140m) per ball; 18–19 sts and 23–25 rows to 4in/10cm in St st using size 8–9 (5–5.5mm) knitting needles.

Kidsilk Haze

A fine-weight mohair mix yarn; 70 percent super kid mohair, 30 percent silk; ☐oz/25g (229yd/210m) per ball; 18–25 sts and 23–34 rows to 4in/10cm in St st using size 3–8 (3.25–5mm) knitting needles.

Lima

A 84 percent baby alpaca, 8 percent merino wool, 8 percent nylon mix yarn; 1¾oz/50g (109yd/100m) per ball; 20 sts and 26 rows to 4in/10cm in St st using size 9 (5.5mm) knitting needles.

Wool Cotton

A wool/cotton blend yarn (50 percent merino wool, 50 percent cotton); 1¾oz/50g (123yd/113m) per ball; 22–24sts and 30–32 rows to 4in/10cm in St st using size 5–6 (3.75–4mm) knitting needles.

Wool Cotton 4ply

A wool/cotton blend yarn (50 percent merino wool, 50 percent cotton); 1¾oz/50g (197yd/180m) per ball; 28 sts and 36 rows to 4in/10cm in St st using size 2 (3.25mm) knitting needles.

RESOURCES

AUSTRALIA: Australian Country Spinners, Pty Ltd, Level 7, 409 St. Kilda Road,Melbourne Vic 3004.
Tel: 03 9380 3888 Fax: 03 9820 0989
Email: customerservice@auspinners.com.au

AUSTRIA: Coats Harlander Ges GmbH, Autokaderstraße 29, BT2, 1.OG, 1210 Wien, Österreich
Tel: 00800 26 27 28 00 Fax: (01) 7644 802 133

BELGIUM: Coats N.V. c/o Coats GmbH Kaiserstr.1 79341 Kenzingen Germany Tel: 0800 77892 Fax: 00 49 7644 802 133
Email: sales.coatsninove@coats.com
Web: www.coatscrafts.be

BULGARIA: Coats Bulgaria, 7 Magnaurska Shkola Str., BG-1784 Sofia, Bulgaria Tel: (+359 2) 976 77 41 Fax: (+359 2) 976 77 20 Email: officebg@coats.com
Web: www.coatsbulgaria.bg

CANADA: Westminster Fibers, 10 Roybridge Gate, Suite 200 Vaughan, Ontario L4H 3M8
Tel: (800) 263-2354 Fax: 905 856 6184
Email: info@westminsterfibers.com

CHINA: Coats Shanghai Ltd, No 9 Building , Baosheng Road, Songjiang Industrial Zone,
Shanghai.Tel: (86- 21) 13816681825 Fax: (86-21) 57743733-326
Email: victor.li@coats.com,

CYPRUS: Coats Bulgaria, 7 Magnaurska Shkola Str., BG-1784 Sofia, Bulgaria Tel: (+359 2) 976 77 41 Fax: (+359 2) 976 77 20 Email: officebg@coats.com
Web: www.coatscrafts.com.cy

ESTONIA: Coats Eesti AS, Ampri tee 9/4, 74001 Viimsi Harjumaa
Tel: +372 630 6250 Fax: +372 630 6260
Email: info@coats.ee Web: www.coatscrafts.co.ee

DENMARK: Coats Expotex AB, S-516 21 Dalsjöfors, Sweden
Tel: (45) 35 83 50 20 E-mail: info.dk@coats.com
FINLAND: Coats Opti Crafts Oy, Huhtimontie 6 04200

KERAVA
Tel: (358) 9 274871 Fax: (358) 9 2748 7330
Email: coatsopti.sales@coats.com
www.coatscrafts.fi

FRANCE: Coats France, c/o Coats GmbH, Kaiserstr.1, 79341 Kenzingen, Germany
Tel: +32 (0) 0810 06 00 02 Email: artsdufil@coats.com Web: www.coatscrafts.fr

GERMANY: Coats GmbH, Kaiserstrasse 1, D-79341 Kenzingen, Germany Tel: (49) 7644 - 802 222 Fax: (49) 7644 - 802 300
Web: www.coatsgmbh.de

GREECE: Coats Bulgaria, 7 Magnaurska Shkola Str., BG-1784 Sofia, Bulgaria Tel: (+359 2) 976 77 41 Fax: (+359 2) 976 77 20 Email: officebg@coats.com Web: www.coatscrafts.gr

HOLLAND: Coats B.V. c/o Coats GmbH Kaiserstr.1 79341 Kenzingen, Germany
Tel: 0800 0226648 Fax: 00 49 7644 802 133 Email: sales. coatsninove@coats.com
Web: www.coatscrafts.be

HONG KONG: East Unity Company Ltd, Unit B2, 7/F., Block B, Kailey Industrial Centre,
12 Fung Yip Street, Chai Wan
Tel: (852)2869 7110 Email: eastunityco@yahoo.com.hk

ICELAND: Storkurinn, Laugavegi 59, 101 Reykjavik
Tel: (354) 551 8258 Email: storkurinn@simnet.is

ITALY: Coats Cucirini srl, viale sarca n∞ 223, 20126 Milano
Tel: 02636151 Fax: 0266111701

KOREA: Coats Korea Co. Ltd, 5F Eyeon B/D, 935-40 Bangbae-Dong, 137-060
Tel: (82) 2 521 6262 Fax: (82) 2 521 5181
Email: rozenpark@coats.com

LATVIA: Coats Latvija SIA, Mukusalas str. 41 b, Riga LV-1004
Tel: +371 7 625173 Fax: +371 7 892758
Email: info@coats.lv Web: www.coatscrafts.lv

LEBANON: y.knot, Saifi Village, Mkhalissiya Street 162, Beirut
Tel: (961) 1 992211 Fax: (961) 1 315553
Email: y.knot@cyberia.net.lb

LITHUANIA & RUSSIA: Coats Lietuva UAB, A. Juozapaviciaus str. 6/2, LT-09310 Vilnius Tel: +370 527 30971 Fax: +370 527 2305
Email: info@coats.lt Web: www.coatscrafts.lt

LUXEMBOURG: Coats N.V. c/o Coats GmbH Kaiserstr.1 79341 Kenzingen, Germany Tel: 00 49 7644 802 222 Fax: 00 49 7644 802 133 Email: sales.coatsninove@coats.com
Web: www.coatscrafts.be

MALTA: John Gregory Ltd, 8 Ta'Xbiex Sea Front, Msida MSD 1512, Malta Tel: +356 2133 0202 Fax: +356 2134 4745
Email: raygreg@onvol.net

MEXICO: Estambres Crochet SA de CV, PO Box SANTAMARIA, 64650 MONTERREY
NEW ZEALAND: ACS New Zealand, 1 March Place, Belfast, Christchurch Tel: 64 3 323 6665 Fax: 64 3 323 6660

NORWAY: Coats Knappehuset AS, Pb 100 Ulset, 5873 Bergen
Tel: (47) 55 53 93 00 Fax: (47) 55 53 93 93
E-mail: kundeservice@coats.com

PORTUGAL: Companhia de Linha Coats & Clark, Quinta de Cravel, 4400 Vilanova de Gaia Portugal
Tel: 00 351 223 770700

SINGAPORE: Golden Dragon Store, 101 Upper Cross Street #02-51, People's Park Centre, Singapore 058357
Tel: (65) 6 5358454 Fax: (65) 6 2216278
Email: gdscraft@hotmail.com

SOUTH AFRICA: Arthur Bales LTD, 62 4th Avenue, Linden 2195
Tel: (27) 11 888 2401 Fax: (27) 11 782 6137
Email: arthurb@new.co.za

SPAIN: Coats Fabra, Sant Adria 20, 08030 Barcelona
Tel: (34) 932908400 Fax: 932908409
Email: atencion.clientes@coats.com

SWEDEN: Coats Expotex AB, Stationsvägen 2, 516 21 Dalsjöfors
Tel: (46) 33 720 79 00 Fax: 46 31 47 16 50
E-mail: kundtjanst@coats.com

SWITZERLAND: Coats Stroppel AG, Postfach 46, 5300 Turgi, Schweiz Tel: (41) 562981220 Fax: (41) 7644-802 133
Web: www.coatscrafts.ch

TAIWAN: Cactus Quality Co Ltd, 7FL-2, No. 140, Sec.2 Roosevelt Rd, Taipei,10084 Taiwan, R.O.C.
Tel: 00886-2-23656527 Fax: 886-2-23656503
Email: cqcl@ms17.hinet.net

THAILAND: Global Wide Trading, 10 Lad Prao Soi 88, Bangkok 10310 Tel: 00 662 933 9019 Fax: 00 662 933 9110
Email: global.wide@yahoo.com

USA: Westminster Fibers Inc, 8 Shelter Drive, Greer, 29650
Tel: (800) 445-9276 Fax: 864-879-9432
Email: info@westminsterfibers.com

UK: Rowan, Green Lane Mill, Holmfirth, West Yorkshire, England HD9 2DX Tel: +44 (0) 1484 681881 Fax: +44 (0) 1484 687920
Email: ccuk.sales@coats.com
Web: www.knitrowan.com

AUTHOR'S ACKNOWLEDGMENTS

I would like to thank my family and friends for their support and for putting up with my scarf obsession while working on this book— especially Mark who has had tape measures and scarves wrapped around him a lot! Thanks also go to Sharon for being such a wonderful person to work with on this project and a huge support generally. Finally, thanks to Susan, Katie, Jen, Darren, and Michael for making this book look so great.

PUBLISHERS' ACKNOWLEDGMENTS

The publishers would like to thanks Sharon Brant for acting as the technical consultant on this book, Darren Brant for the layouts, Michael Wicks for model photography and Darren Brant for techniques photography, Katie Hardwicke for editing, Jen Arnall-Culliford for the charts, and Marilyn Wilson for checking the patterns.

They would also like to thank Kimberley and Heida (Nevs Model Agency) and Hannah for modelling and the Barn Theatre, Welwyn, for the hire of the studio.